"*Great book. Thank you for your fresh approach Cam.*"
- **Janine Allis,** founder and CEO, Boost Juice

"*I knew what I wanted to say. Cam refocused me on how to say it in a way that cut straight to the heart. That made all the difference. This man knows what he's doing.*"
- **Andrew Denton,** Journalist and Media Personality

"*This is an outstanding book. The core premise certainly worked for me, and I believe you have nailed it for people making major presentations.*"
- **Paul Thompson,** founder of both Austereo and DMG (now Nova Entertainment).

"*Cam gives you a philosophy that frees you to be yourself and simple tools to structure your ideas so you engage your audience.*"
- **Verne Harnish,** CEO of Gazelles and author of *Scaling Up* (*Rockefeller Habits 2.0*).

"*Cam has helped us enormously in getting our ideas across.*"
- **Alastair Clarkson,** 4-time Premiership Coach, Hawthorn Football Club

"*The Vivid Method has helped me to bring order to the world of information chaos - in the media, at the lectern and the board table. The secret to confident and powerful delivery skills is clarity. Read the book!*"
- **Mark Evans,** AFL Football Operations Manager.

"*3 years ago I had a mortal fear of public speaking that was holding me back in my career. Now I actually enjoy it! Since working with Cam I have been the keynote speaker at several conferences around the world.*"
- **Sam Cavanagh,** National Executive Producer – Southern Cross Austereo and keynote Speaker at RadioDays Europe 2013 / 2014 / 2015.

D1637397

What's your message?

Public speaking with twice the impact,
using half the effort

Cam Barber

First published in 2015
By Vivid Learning Pty Ltd
PO Box 6468, Melbourne 3004, Victoria, Australia
www.vividmethod.com
Email: events@vividmethod.com

What's Your Message? Public Speaking with twice the impact, using half the effort
© Cam Barber 2015

ISBN 978-0-9925055-0-9 (paperback)
ISBN 978-0-9925055-1-6 (EPUB)
ISBN 978-0-9925055-2-3 (Mobipocket)
ISBN 978-0-9925055-3-0 (PDF ebook)

National Library of Australia Cataloguing-in-Publication entry
Author: Barber, Cam, author.
Title: What's your message : public speaking with twice the impact, using half the effort / Cam Barber.

Subjects: Public speaking--Handbooks, manuals, etc.
Oral communication--Handbooks, manuals, etc.
Oratory--Handbooks, manuals, etc.

Dewey Number: 808.51

Contents

JUST BEFORE WE GET STARTED...

My friend Michael is sitting across the table from me. He's the CEO of a major entertainment company. We have just finished the outline for his presentation. He sits back in his chair looking satisfied.

Then his energy changes and concern takes over his face.

He says, 'The planning feels complete, Cam. My message is clear and the structure looks good, but that's not my biggest challenge. It's the START! The real problem is that awkward feeling just before I speak. My throat is tight and I wonder if I'll stumble on my words. And, at the start of any talk, there's that echoing silence and all those expressionless faces wondering where you're going to take them. It takes a while to build a good rhythm."

The start can be a challenge for all of us. The beginning of a speech is a point-in-time that's full of uncertainty (and uncertainty is the root cause of anxiety, but we'll get to that later). We walk on stage and there's this energy vacuum and the audience looking at us to fill it. It can be difficult to think clearly with all those expectant eyes on us, and the way we manage those moments can determine how the rest of the presentation goes.

Then Michael said, "Cam, tell me how I can eliminate the start of a speech!"

And that was the day we did it. We devised a way to **eliminate the awkward start of any speech**.

He was half-joking of course. But we brainstormed it that afternoon, and we did it. Not possible you say? Surely every speech needs a start... Well, we vanquished it - and you can too. We found a way to not only eliminate the awkward start of a speech, but achieve 4 crucial goals:

1. Reduce anxiety.

2. Convert the cold mood of any room, hall or stadium into a warm conversational energy.

3. Take the spotlight off your *performance* so you can relax.

4. Create an environment to engage your audience.

It's an incredibly powerful technique that works with any audience or any subject. It puts you instantly in control of the room, while taking most of the traditional public speaking pressures off you. It works if you are a quiet, thoughtful, softly spoken introvert-style speaker - or a loud, fast, dynamic extrovert-style -or anything in between. It works no matter how much sleep you had the night before.

This powerful technique is called 'Just before we get started...'

In a nutshell, the first words you say are,

'Just before we get started...'

...followed by a few words on something you have prepared to chat about. Like the background to your talk; or your role; or the beginning of the relationship that led to your talk; or housekeeping issues (like how long you'll speak for, how to manage questions, if there is a handout), or anything you like.

The point is, by using the words '***before*** we get started...' you release the pressure of the start. The energy vacuum is filled and you've done it with a conversational tone.

Of course, technically you *have* started, but after your relaxed intro, you simply continue on with your talk as planned. This avoids the drama of a traditional start. The 'just-before-we-get-started' technique works like magic. Amazing, but true. Try it for yourself. I'll explain exactly how this works later as it's one of the techniques covered in the 'Give Great Explanations' section at the end of the book.

First, let's look at how this book is structured.

...Oh, and if you're still reading, it looks like the 'just-before-we-get-started' technique works to open a *book* as well. :)

How this book is structured

This book has 2 parts...

The first part is called 'The Power of Messaging'. It shares examples that demonstrate that a compelling message is the lynchpin to great public speaking. These examples are from great leaders, sporting professionals, CEOs of business and non-profit organisations, scientists, book authors, salespeople, project managers, radio stars, TV show hosts, and a range of other roles. Some examples are from people who inspire me, while others are my clients. They illustrate the incredible benefits of being able to deliver a *transferable* message.

The second part shows you a 3-part method to prepare and deliver great speeches and presentations. It's called 'The Vivid Method for Public Speaking' and we've taught it to over 15,000 people. The 3 parts follow a specific sequence and help you think clearly, prepare in less time, dissolve nerves effortlessly, engage your audience from start to finish and leave them with a memorable message. The 3 parts of the Vivid Method are:

1. The 5 principles that help you think clearly and control nerves.

2. The Speech Outline process that helps you clarify and structure ideas.

3. A range of options to give great explanations.

Why another book on public speaking?

I've been reading and collecting books on public speaking and presentation skills for 20 years, and wondered if the world needed another. It does. Why? Because most of the books and, ultimately, most of the training in public speaking, is based on a bad idea.

The idea is that there's an *optimum* way to 'be' when speaking in public. That we should adjust our body language, control our gestures, restrict (or exaggerate) our facial expressions and basically fit into a cookie-cutter, mechanical style to achieve this 'optimum'.

It's a dumb idea and it doesn't work. It implies you have to change who you are, which wastes a tremendous amount of energy and actually *creates an environment for anxiety*. In this stressful situation, speakers use far more effort than if they were just able to speak as themselves.

I learnt this the hard way. I was told that my style was wrong and I needed to change it if I was going to be an effective speaker (this story is explained in 'Principle 4: Natural Style'). After banging my head against a wall trying to follow the advice I was given, I finally developed a new approach based on **message recall** and **natural style.** It frees people from the shackles and misdirection of the traditional 'performance' approach.

There appears to be a desperate need for this new method for 3 reasons. Firstly, speakers regularly fail to deliver a clear message, so they waste their opportunity in front of an audience. Secondly, people who have great ideas don't share them because they get lost in information overload (inability to easily sort their ideas) or a fear of public speaking. Finally, more than half the trainers teaching public speaking to businesspeople today are actors, so this 'performance' approach continues to spread like a virus.

So, I offer you a method for public speaking that is simple, reduces preparation time, requires less practice and gives you twice the impact with half the effort. My hope is that it will help you bring your ideas to life.

I've taught this method at conferences, coaching sessions and in longer training courses, and one of life's pleasures is when people come up and explain how it has completely changed their perspective - that it transforms a difficult problem into a simple step-by-step process.

In fact, people who ask questions with a furrowed brow at the start of a session, often give feedback at the end of a session like, 'Huh, you know, it's just common sense really, isn't it?'

This is a wonderful compliment.

You might think it would be nicer to hear something like, 'Wow, you must be so clever', or 'you have so many good ideas' or 'those dramatic techniques are amazing'. But when people come to the conclusion that the method is just *common sense*, we have achieved something much more powerful. It means they find it so **easy to apply** that they use it without making dramatic changes to their life, and without having to spend years developing their skills.

This method can make you a great speaker, today. (If you start reading in the early morning, that is. Otherwise, I guess we are talking about tomorrow or maybe the weekend...)

THE POWER
OF
MESSAGING

A STATISTICAL ANOMALY

The sequence of events that led to this book started with a presentation course I attended 20 years ago. It was terrible. It told me I had to have acting skills and fit into a cookie-cutter mould.

This training, which I had hoped would improve my public speaking skills, actually made me **more nervous** and much **more self-conscious** in front of an audience. For example, if '6 gestures per minute' was optimum, as we were told, then my natural style was *10 times wrong*, because the facilitator showed a video of me to the group doing *60* gestures a minute. My extroverted style didn't fit the 'optimum' (more on this in the 'Myths' section).

The year of living frustrated

But I didn't know any better so I tried to **change my style** and follow the rules I was taught, banging my head against the wall for almost a year. It was frustrating. I was a sales manager who made business presentations on a daily basis. I constantly felt inadequate. The harder I tried to fit the mould they offered as the 'right way', the worse I became.

During that year of frustration, I started to observe great speakers. The best speaker I knew personally was Paul Thompson, my CEO at the time. Paul Thompson is a legend in Australian Broadcasting. He founded both the Austereo and the Nova radio networks *from scratch*. He's been described as a visionary leader and most people who've worked with him would say he's a great operator and a motivational force.

First, break all the rules

What was striking about Paul Thompson's public speaking is that he broke all the rules that we were taught in the course. He had few-to-no gestures. He was an introvert-style who had a slight 'tick' when he spoke (did you know that both Winston Churchill and Jack Welch had to deal with a stutter they both had since childhood?). Paul's 'tick' was a half-cough, half throat-clear every 20 seconds or so. And he bounced on his toes in an awkward way!

However, none of this mattered. He was able to capture the room, engage us from start to finish and deliver a compelling message that motivated the entire organisation. So I asked myself, what was the main thing I could learn from Paul Thompson's public speaking style? The answer was, a clear and memorable message.

I can still recall the messages from his major speeches. They made so much sense. The performance techniques (that the training course spent sooo much time teaching us) didn't seem to matter. He was able to appear genuine and believable without using them. He didn't need to follow 'the rules' to be a great speaker.

But this was just my personal observation. The training course had hard research to back up their rules. Who was I to disagree? (Later I found out that the 'hard research' was taken out of context and what they were teaching was in many cases the *opposite* of what the researcher had concluded!! More on this in the 'myths' section.)

A turning point

It was around this time that I came across an article in *Fortune* magazine about the 2 most effective CEOs in the world at the time. It had a profound effect on me, and reinforced the idea that **messaging** was the vital and fundamental heart of every great speaker. The article was published on December 11, 1995, and talked about how the CEOs of Coca Cola and General Electric had unlocked the secrets of creating shareholder value.

Fortune had decided to rank the most successful companies in the Fortune 500 based on a new measure. The article starts with, 'There are all sorts of ways to grade a chief executive...' Then they list 6 or 7 ways, but decide on a measure called MVA or 'market value added'. MVA asks: 'What is the difference between the cash that investors have put into a business over its lifetime and the amount they could get out of it today by selling their shares?'

So *Fortune* put together a list of all the major companies in America and ranked them by MVA. They were shocked by the results. Two companies stood out in what would normally be called a statistical anomaly.

Don Bradman is a statistical anomaly

What's a statistical anomaly? It's when something falls way outside the normal range. For example, a freakishly good result like cricket legend Donald Bradman. His batting average is 99.96. That means every single time he went out to bat, he averaged almost 100 runs. So, how does this compare with all the other greats in history? Well, as of today, incorporating 150 years of cricketing data, the next best have batting averages ranging between 50 and 61 runs. There are dozens of incredible batsmen that fall into that range. The numbers get lower from there. So to have someone with an average of almost 100 is a freak. It's 65% higher than the cluster of the next best. Statisticians will often eliminate this 'statistical anomaly' to better show the *truth* in the data.

Well, in the *Fortune* article there were 2 results that can be considered statistical anomalies. They were both about 65% higher than the cluster of the next best on the list. After looking at 16 years of growth using an MVA calculation, Coca Cola was number 1 with a ranking of 61 and GE was number 2, with 52. And, as *Fortune* reported, 'No other company came close. Walmart, in 3rd place, had 35 in MVA, Merck, 32, and Microsoft, 30', etc. So you can see there is a similar cluster of great operators in the 30-35 range and 2 outliers that were about 65% better.

Leaders with opposite personalities

The CEO of GE was Jack Welch and the CEO of Coke was Roberto Goizueta (whose most enduring quote, by the way, is 'Communication is the only task you cannot delegate'). These men had opposite personalities and completely different leadership styles. What was their secret?

Roberto was an immigrant with a quiet, measured personality, he was always polite, didn't like open confrontation, liked a predictable schedule and never seemed to take off his suit jacket.

Jack Welch, on the other hand, was hot-headed, impulsive, charming, proud of his heavy drinking fraternity days, loved a fight and was most comfortable in his shirt sleeves.

And their businesses also couldn't have been more different. Coke is essentially a one-product company and GE is a conglomerate that sells thousands of products. Coke sells image, GE sells performance.

Ironically, they became chairmen and CEO of their companies around the same time, just a month apart in 1981. Both Coke and GE were in trouble when they took the helm. For example, GE's manufacturing-based businesses were being killed by the Japanese obsession with quality. Both businesses had lost focus. Coke had been losing market share for nearly 20 years.

Unlocking the secret of great CEOs

So my question was, is there a common theme? Is there a quality they both had? A single competence or talent that generated stellar results even though they had dramatically different businesses and different styles? There was! Messaging. Both men's standout quality was their ability to sell ideas by making them clear and memorable.

As Fortune put it, both men came up with a game plan and basically said, 'We're going to change the way we run these businesses and here's how we're going to do it. They figured out what they needed to do. Then told their employees. And then they did it - relentlessly'.

Does that sound game-changing? Maybe not at first glance, but let's look more closely. The common theme was that both men were able to create a strategy and *communicate it so effectively* that the entire company executed magnificently. Both men isolated a vivid message that drove the business for decades.

They were messaging experts.

Roberto's key message

The Coke message was:

> "We now have one key measure of success, <u>return on capital</u>, no matter what part of the business you are in."

He explained that the key to success is *efficient allocation of capital*. And the way to succeed is to employ this one simple formula. In other words, "You borrow money at a certain rate and invest it at a higher rate and pocket the difference". This gave all of his managers a principle that allowed them to make a range of decisions without Roberto's approval, but that followed his core principle. It worked like a charm.

"Nobody had taken the time to explain what our cost of capital was … when you explain those things, intelligent people will eventually come to their senses," Roberto said. If people "don't know where they're going, I mean, you don't want them to get there very fast" he added.

Roberto produced little brochures explaining how powerful this principle was and gave examples of how it worked. He visited all of his senior managers personally and, in his low-key style, talked about *return on capital*. He leant over desks, chatted over meals, pulled out his folksy brochures and made sure that everybody understood his message. It was even outlined in annual reports to all shareholders.

This beautifully simple message allowed Roberto to delegate power while giving everybody a laser-like focus on his strategy. In the beginning, the stock market didn't understand what was going on. They saw Coca Cola making 'strange' decisions that caused them to let go of their Triple-A debt rating and borrow more money than was thought prudent at the time. But Coke knew exactly what they were doing with the money they were borrowing because every project was meticulously assessed on return on capital.

Jack's key message

Jack Welch also used a simple message to drive change and delegate authority, yet keep his massive conglomerate focused. His message was that each business in the GE group needed to be number 1 or number 2 in their global marketplace in 18 months. If they were number 3, 4 or lower, these businesses would be sold or closed. Imagine this. The new CEO pulls all the executives together and delivers this simple message:

"Look at the business you run. You either have to be number 1 or 2, or we will sell you or shut you down. If you are not 1 or 2 now, either make a plan to do so or create a plan to sell or close down your business."

Again, this simple message created an 'invisible hand' that guided hundreds of individual decisions by senior managers at GE. It worked incredibly well.

The sharp end of communication

Ok, we've been told '*communication is important*' before. But what does that actually mean? These examples showed that there should be a specific focus for communication. A vivid message.

This was a turning point for me. It cut through the noise of personality style, leadership style, delivery skills and so on. And it was true for an audience of 1 or 1,000.

These 2 messages (and the CEOs driving them) created a rocket under both Coke and GE in the early 80s that continued to fuel both businesses into the mid-90s when the *Fortune* article was written, and underpinned a level of success that was 65% better than the world's next best. The messages convinced the tradition-bound bureaucracies to accept change and gave them a clear focus for their energies.

So, it seemed that style was irrelevant when it came to results. I mean, of course a person's style has an impact. It's integral. But style is not the driver, it's simply part of the package. The real impact across an organisation came from absolute clarity.

This helped me realise that the public speaking training I had attended had the focus back-to-front. So I started a consulting business to put it right. We developed training that placed *message* and *natural style* first, and allowed the 'performance' and 'style' to flow effortlessly from clarity. In the beginning we called it ClarityFirst, prioritising the ability to think clearly and structure ideas. It later became known as the Vivid Method for Public Speaking.

ONE PRESENTATION CAN DEFINE A CAREER

Sometimes the trajectory of a career can be defined by a single 30-minute talk. Unfortunately, what many of us have been taught about public speaking stifles our thinking, adds to our anxiety and sends us in the wrong direction.

One of my early coaching clients, Joe, was president of Paramount Pictures in Japan. He had to fly to Los Angeles to outline his plan to promote a big new film, *War of the Worlds*. He, along with similar executives from around the world, would be presenting to Paramount's senior executives as well as the heads of both Tom Cruise's and Steven Spielberg's production companies.

He needed to change the existing view

But this wasn't a run-of-the-mill presentation. Joe was under pressure following his division's poor performance over the previous year, including a disappointing result with another Tom Cruise movie, *Collateral*. There was a perception that he and his team were disorganised. His audience would be sceptical about his ability to deliver on the new film. In short, Joe's presentation needed to change their existing view and give them full confidence in his abilities.

It was Joe's boss in Singapore who called me in to help.

"Joe knows his stuff," he told me, "and he has a great team, but he's not convincing in public speaking situations. He often becomes flustered when interrupted with a question – which will happen a lot in this meeting. He seems to freeze a little under the spotlight, and get lost in the details."

The reality was, Joe's job was on the line. When I first met with Joe he was clearly stressed. He talked about his PowerPoint slides first, "We have 5 people pulling together slides across 3 countries. There are 70 slides so far, and more to come." He seemed overwhelmed just talking about the quantity of information. "Ok, apart from the slides, how do you feel about the presentation?" I asked.

Joe let out a sigh, "I have all this conflicting advice bouncing around in my head. I know I don't present very well, even though I've attended presentation courses in the past. And well-meaning people keep giving me advice; how to stand, how to gesture, how to speak – but keeping all those rules in mind while trying to get through all my slides can turn my mind to mud."

The Al Gore story

I decided to tell Joe a story about Al Gore. Al Gore is well known for 3 things: His movie *An Inconvenient Truth* – one of the most successful documentaries of all time; his 8-year Vice Presidency alongside Bill Clinton; and his close but unsuccessful campaign for the US Presidency against George W. Bush in 2000.

During this Presidential campaign, Gore was criticised for giving wooden and uninspiring speeches. Ironically, the best speech of his campaign was his concession speech … *after* he had lost and the election campaign was over. In that speech, he appeared far more relaxed than during the entire campaign, coming across as both natural and believable. It was this 'real' version of Gore who would succeed so well in the years to come as a speaker.

A few years ago I was fortunate enough to meet and chat with Bill Clinton, and asked him about these two different Al Gores. Clinton said, "It drove me nuts" watching Gore communicate during the campaign because he knew he could be so much better. He also shared his view that the invention of the electric microphone changed forever the criteria for public speaking - overacting is no longer needed.

The problem for Al Gore was that too many 'experts' had become involved in his campaign. They coached him on how to speak, act and gesture - including many of the rules Joe had been given. They advised him on specific words he should (and shouldn't) use based on market research. They even steered him away from the subject he was most passionate about: the environment.

First, kill all the consultants!

As Joe Klein noted in his 2006 book *Politics Lost*, the consultants never considered that Gore's best opportunity to win was to be real. (I *love* that *Fortune* magazine titled their review of Klein's book, 'First, kill all the consultants'!)

Many people have wondered if Gore might have won that knife-edge election had he spoken more naturally and ignored the too-clever advice from his consultants. We will never know. But the story illustrates the lost opportunities that can result from misguided advice about communication.

Joe liked the Al Gore example. "So, I should ignore all that confusing advice and just be myself? How do I know that will get the best result? And how will I deal with the nerves?"

"Relax and find the pace that allows you to breathe comfortably." I responded. "Then you'll be able to think clearly when you speak. That's your foundation. On top of that we'll structure your ideas and identify key messages".

From that point on, Joe and I focused on 2 main things: 1) the clarity of his messages, and 2) getting comfortable with his natural style.

His presentation in Los Angeles rocked! It *exceeded* his own expectations and those of his managers. He was relaxed and confident, speaking with certainty throughout. He didn't try to be more dramatic or extroverted than he was. He handled tough questions with assurance – because he had anticipated them in his preparation. Far from being flustered and uncertain, Joe was seen as the best presenter from all the countries at the meeting. The end result was that his $22 million plan was accepted – and his career trajectory was once again looking up.

Joe's story is not unique. Conflicting advice, concerns about having too much to say, anxiety about presenting in the 'right way' – perhaps even a career held back: these are common experiences. Perhaps you can relate to some?

A message is the doorway to an idea

Fortunately, there is a better way. It's possible to **speak with certainty,** and **persuade with clarity**. It starts with your message, which is the *doorway to* *your idea.* It's the hook that draws people in to the details. It's the summary that can be recalled easily, allowing more information to be remembered. A good message becomes the afterglow of your talk; the thing that is shared and repeated. A vivid message is the magic that brings your ideas to life.

Now, let's have a look at a case study of a professional sporting club and how vivid messages across their organisation have helped them become so successful.

MESSAGING CASE STUDY: PROFESSIONAL FOOTBALL CLUBS

Few people outside Australia are familiar with AFL Football, the game many call *Australian Rules*. It's a shame. AFL (Australian Football League) Football is the most fun and exciting game played anywhere in the world. And even though it's only played in Australia, AFL football has the 4th highest attendance of any sport in the world - an average of 32,436 people per game - a bigger average crowd than Major League Baseball.

After a few years teaching this new public speaking method, I got a call from the President of the Hawthorn Football Club, Jeff Kennett. If you haven't heard of him, Jeff is a larger-than-life character in Australia. A former politician, he was a high-profile Premier of Victoria.

Jeff was interested in media training for players, coaches and the executive team at Hawthorn. It was funny though. I'd never spoken to him and had no reason to believe he knew about me.

When I got back to the office after a meeting, my assistant simply said, "Someone named Jeff called, he left a mobile number, I'm not sure what he wants". I said, "Mmm, do *I* need to speak to him, if it's a general enquiry can't you handle it?" I wondered if it was another caller with 20 questions about public speaking but no plans for business. I called the number anyway, the voice answered "Yes?" and I responded, in a tone trailing off into a question, "This is Cam Barber, returning your call...".

Jeff has a loud, distinctive voice and a strong presence. He said, "HELLO CAM, THIS IS JEFF KENNETT".

"Oh! Um, hello Jeff, (I spontaneously stood up from my chair. It was weird, I felt too informal sitting down, even on the phone) how can I help you?"

Anyway, we had a chat about the club's needs, which led to a program of coaching and training, and a relationship with the club that has lasted 8 years so far. I've worked with 3 other AFL clubs as well and it's been very interesting to observe the importance of communication skills on the success of professional sporting clubs.

For example, Hawthorn Football Club is regularly referred to as the '*most professional*' club in the competition. But this didn't just happen. That branding was consciously created. And it's part of the reason they have been so successful over the last 8 years. Let's have a look at how it works...

External messages

Hawthorn Football Club has dominated the AFL competition since 2008. The word most commonly associated with Hawthorn over the last 8 years is 'professional'. In fact, if you read a week or 2 of sports commentary, you'll usually see a few references to the Hawks' professionalism.

This is not an accident...

In early 2007 I conducted a Messaging project with the Hawks' administration (Coach, CEO, Football Manager, Communications Manager, COO, etc) to get agreement on the key messages to represent the club. The top-level message agreed on that day was:

'We aim to be the most professional club in the competition'.

This message was dropped into as many conversations with the media as possible. It also guided management and the playing group internally, as well as driving communication to members and fans via the website.

The *sub message* in 2007 was, "...and we've made some bold decisions to get there, and we'll keep making the tough decisions (because the only way to succeed is to be the most professional club...)". The sub-messages are updated each year as situations change.

The idea behind this 'Message Hierarchy' is that you have:
• Clarity about where you want media conversations to go
• Great flexibility because it's not a script to repeat robotically.
These messages are the essence of living conversations. They guide the

speaker and give them the freedom to explain ideas and answer questions from their own perspective. Head coach, Alastair Clarkson, said in 2012 'Cam Barber's messaging strategy keeps everybody on the same page'.

Port Adelaide: 'We will never, ever give up'

There are other recent examples of a message driving success for AFL clubs. For example, Port Adelaide's current message is:

'We will never, ever give up'.

This message coincided with a dramatic turnaround in less than 12 months. In post-game media interviews, Coach Ken Hinkley regularly referred to this message as part of the reason they won.

How did Port Adelaide's message come about? At the start of 2013, Port President David Koch was told by his sister that she was thinking about giving up her membership of the once-great club. She told him she couldn't stand watching games where the team gave up and lost without really trying. She wasn't the only one. Membership numbers were poor. So Koch, chose the 'never, ever give up' message to drive the membership marketing from that point.

Within 6 months, the message had resonated with players and supporters alike. And the winning started. Port Adelaide made a dramatic turnaround from bottom of the ladder to finals contender - often dominating *the last quarter* to secure the win.

Fremantle Dockers: 'Anyone, anywhere, anytime'

Fremantle Football Club have done very well over the last few years guided by their message:

'Anyone, Anywhere, Anytime'.

Like Port Adelaide, this message was also crafted to address a specific challenge for the club. Based in Perth, Fremantle had to travel greater distances than any other club to play their games. The win/loss record showed that Fremantle was less successful when they traveled to play away from Perth.

So, what's the message coach Ross Lyon chose? *'Anyone, anywhere, anytime'*. It worked. Fremantle won their first final away from home that year. One sportswriter described the message as "an encapsulation of their philosophy under coach Ross Lyon. A galvanising message can make a team feel like they are on a mission."

The power and effectiveness of these 3 simple words has helped build inspiration and commitment in the Fremantle team.

Internal messages (to players and staff)

Of course, messaging doesn't work if you don't live it. In Hawthorn's case, they live 'professional'. Although, the messaging can help with that as well. It can be used as a constant reminder that drives everyone's behaviour.

The right message conveys 'who we are' as a club. It helps build an identity for an organisation. This identity is the foundation of leadership. My former CEO, Paul Thompson, felt it was a leader's *obligation* to provide this kind of identity and clarity of purpose. It not only gives people a clear reason to come to work, it aligns and focuses their energies.

This makes the organisation more effective *and* the workplace more enjoyable! On the other hand, lack of clarity creates confusion, frustration and uncertainty. Clear messaging reduces these energy-sapping menaces.

The Hawks message aspiring to be "the most professional club in the competition" is often used by journalists and commentators as *a conclusion they came to themselves.* They've heard the message (many times) and they've seen the professional behaviour, so it just comes together in their mind. It's the same inside the club. That's how good messaging works. It focuses your energy and leverages the support of others.

'If you're good enough, you're old enough'

Messaging underpins success in all sports. In European football, Sir Matt Busby, who managed Manchester United to great success between 1945 and 1971, crafted many timeless messages. His quote, *'If you're good enough, you're old enough'* is still on the wall in the Manchester United player's dressing room.

We don't have to invent new messages, either. There's nothing wrong with appropriating a message that works for your situation. For example, the St Kilda Football Club finished 2014 on the bottom of the league table. Most commentators suggested that St Kilda would finish 2015 on the bottom as well, because the team was full of young, unproven players. The consensus was that they wouldn't win a game and it would take 2-3 years for these players to be good enough to compete at the highest level.

Unless someone introduces new messaging, the consensus view of the media becomes the dominant idea the players are exposed to.

So, imagine you're the new coach of St Kilda. What message do you want to drive home in the pre-season? How about *'If you're good enough, you're old enough'*?

Good choice. Not only does this counteract the negative messaging in the media, it focuses everyone on the goal: get good enough. This message provides clarity for players, direction for supporters and guidance to coaching staff.

This is one of the key messages head coach Alan Richardson has focused on. He supported this with; *"We will judge players on what we see and the way they perform, not their birth certificate. We need to raise expectations and be much more consistent with our performance."*

Halfway into the 2015 season, commentators are now 'surprised at the successes of this young team'.

Leadership messaging can drive behaviour

So we see that many of the most successful teams are associated with vivid messages. The question might be then: is it the messages that help make clubs successful by galvanising energy and focusing attention? Or is it simply that successful sporting clubs know how important messaging is and they include that as part of their operation?

Perhaps it's a bit of both. But what really matters is the evidence to show that leadership messages, when done well, have a powerful ability to drive the behaviour and decision-making that lead to success. Everyone is aligned with the vision, and it unites people across different areas of the club.

The 'glue' that holds the team plan together

In July 2011, commentator Gary Lyon wrote an article about the new style of play introduced by Alastair Clarkson in 2007 that became known as the 'press' or 'Clarko's Cluster'. (http://www.theage.com.au/afl/afl-news/touch-of-greatness-20110701-1guz5.html)

The article was titled 'A touch of greatness' and focused on 2 things:

1. This new style of play significantly changed the game of AFL football.

2. This new style of play would have failed if the team did not execute perfectly.

It's the **execution** of ideas that makes them great. And it's impossible to have team execution without great communication skills. All new ideas require explanation and education to become reality.

The 'stolen' grand final of 2008

Lyon's article stated up front "Hawthorn's largely unexpected premiership back in 2008 was one of the great coaching performances of the modern era." His point is that Clarkson needed to convince his team to abandon the tactics they had used their whole playing lives.

In the lead up to the Grand Final, Clarkson banned the press and public from attending training sessions to practice the new plays. The existing idea that each player had one direct opponent and was held accountable for that opponent was replaced by the idea that players should take defensive responsibility for an area of the playing field.

Every player needed to understand their role

In order for the new 'press' or 'cluster' to work, each player had to understand their role perfectly. As Garry Lyon noted, Clarkson had to overcome the 'not my man, not my fault' mentality to successfully sell the new idea to his players.

This was no easy task. Some of the early strategy meetings the players attended were 2 hours long. It's difficult for professional sports teams to focus mentally on new ideas when their bodies are already exhausted from hours of physical practice.

My suggestions to the Hawks coaching team were to restructure the ideas to make them easier to digest (chunk them), and keep the theory sessions to 60 minutes or less. The simpler an idea appears, the easier it is to execute.

Ideas are useless without great execution

As Lyon explains: "Coming up with a rather radical game plan or concept is only half the battle" because "any time the 'press' broke down, and it did, regularly, in the early days, the Hawks got belted". If just one player failed to execute his role precisely (whether it be lack of concentration or lack of belief in the concept), Clarko's brilliant cluster became a noose around the team's neck.

Clarkson's ability to communicate his message and persuade his players to commit to the new plan, was **the glue that held the team plan together**. The Hawks players executed that plan with complete trust and belief in what Clarkson had coached. This new plan was a great success. It forced all the other teams to adjust their strategies, and helped the Hawks pull off the surprise premiership win in 2008 (and 2 more since then).

Clarkson also used a clever message to motivate the team on the day of the grand final...

Game-day motivational messages

The game-day motivational message has a mythological ingredient to it. We see motivational speeches in movies like 'Coach Carter' (with Samuel L. Jackson), 'Cool Runnings' ("Look in the mirror and tell me what you see"), 'Miracles' (about the US Ice Hockey win at 1980 Olympics) and battlefield speeches like Braveheart ("They may take our lives, but they'll never take away our freedom!"), Gladiator ("What we do in life, echoes in eternity"), even Nelson Mandela's speech to the Captain of the World Cup rugby team ("How do we inspire ourselves to greatness, when nothing else will do?"). The life-changing motivational speech by the coach can have a bit of magic to it.

Actually, the reality is that the coach has to do this *every* game. It's a difficult job to keep coming up with new and interesting ideas to motivate the players. The challenge is that players feel like they've 'heard all this stuff before' and the message doesn't have the impact needed to win.

Alistair Clarkson has shown a great skill for identifying and conveying just the right message at the right time.

The coach's message 2008: 'The shark metaphor'

The Hawks weren't given much chance to win in 2008. It was only Clarkson's 3rd year as a senior coach and the Geelong Cats were highly favoured to win, having lost only 1 game the entire season. It was certainly his most important pre-match speech.

We are used to the image of a football coach shouting and swearing to pump the players up, sometimes asking for impossible, if not illogical, commitment - like 150% effort, no, 200% effort!! But Clarkson had something more powerful than that. An idea supported by the power of metaphor. An idea that focused and motivated the team. An idea that made sense, aligned with the game plan and was **simple enough to recall** - and therefore, guide the player's actions on the day.

Here's what happened. On Grand Final day, the Hawthorn team entered the coach's room to find an outline of a shark on the whiteboard.

The situation was this: the Geelong team had great *forward momentum* and if you gave them an inch they would move the ball quickly and score. So the Hawks had to try to stop this momentum by limiting Geelong's ability to run freely in straight lines.

They had to force Geelong to play wide, sapping the energy from their traditional game. But everybody knew this. What Clarkson did was get that extra focus and effort from the players by likening the Geelong team to a shark.

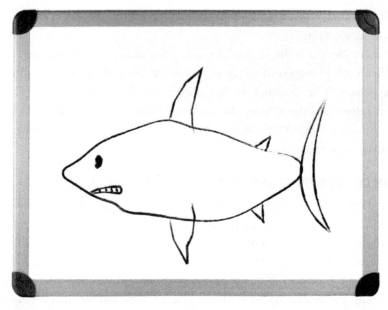

Clarkson explained that sharks must have forward momentum because as soon as they stop, they die. Which is true. Sharks must continually have water moving through their gills or they die. They must keep moving.

"This Geelong team is the same. If you stop them moving, their game will die" said Clarkson.

He did not raise his voice, but there was an urgency to his speech. Then he linked his message to the training and game plan they already knew. (Remember, a vivid message acts as a doorway to more information.) "You don't need to do anything special. You know what will do it today? Just doing it over and over and over – your role – as well as you can, on as many occasions as you can, throughout the course of the game when the opportunity presents" he said.

"They are trying to come through us like a shark," he said. "Good luck to them. [We are] the best defensive pressure side in the competition."

The shark metaphor worked its *magic*. The Hawks beat Geelong to win the Premiership Cup that year, in what was called the 'Stolen Grand Final'.

Making the world less stressful, one space at a time.

bt seemed to be owed to Geelong as a result of
Final win, which led to a Hawthorn loss every
for the next 5 years.
he Kennett Curse.
d when the Geelong players made a private pact
s to 'never to lose to Hawthorn again', and was
t of the 2009 season when Hawks President Jeff
ned the commitment of the Geelong players.
ram he said, "They don't have the psychological
n Geelong when it matters".

The curse seemed real when you watched the games. Following Kennett's comments, Geelong proceeded to defeat Hawthorn in eleven successive matches. Nine of these games were agonisingly close. On more than one occasion, a miraculous score was kicked *after* the final siren. This 11-match winning streak against the Hawks is the longest by any team following a Grand Final loss to their opponent.

Commentators constantly discussed it, betting websites advised of the phenomenon, video parodies abounded and a Sports program employed a wizard, a steaming cauldron and Kennett voodoo doll in an attempt to break it.

Whatever sorcery was at play, this curse needed to be broken if Hawthorn were to win another Grand Final.

The Coach's message 2013: 'The white line'

To reach the 2013 Grand Final, Hawthorn had to beat Geelong in the Preliminary Final the week before. Clarkson crafted another vivid message to motivate the players and bring out that extra level of focus.

As the players walked into the room, a few noticed the large packet of *Black & Gold* plain flour near the lectern. Clarkson stabbed the packet with a knife, and poured it out on the ground to form a thick white line about 5 metres long.

Instead of sitting and listening to the pre-game address as they normally did, nearly every player got out of their seat to see what was happening.

The white line meant 2 things. Firstly, the metaphorical impact associated with the term 'crossing the line' - it means a challenge or a turning point; and second, the actual white line the players cross when they run out onto the field.

Let's face it, both teams are filled with elite and professional athletes. Both teams are focused, committed and drilled in their respective game plans. It is the elusive *extra level of focus*, clarity and engagement that can make the difference between winning and losing. This is what the 'white line' message was designed to access.

The coach started talking about the transformation needed from each person when they ran out onto the field the next day. He noted that the room was full of good people, some of whom were so gentle off the field, they 'wouldn't hurt a fly'.

Then he said, "Winning great contests requires a personality change. When you cross the fabled white line you have to become different people" to commit to whatever it takes (within the rules) to secure victory. Like warriors going into battle.

Clarkson's basic message was not new of course, but his use of metaphor made it stand out. All great leaders know they need to repackage their key messages to keep people focused.

This message was so clever though. Because there is an *actual physical white line* the players cross as they run onto the ground on game day. The coach's references to it worked as a powerful, emotional memory-hook, that opened a mental doorway to the rest of the plan.

Winning the mental game

It also gave the players a valuable second idea; they could stay calm and relaxed until they got to the game. The warrior mentality was only needed after the line was crossed. This helped to maintain mental and physical energy levels. (I've seen many speakers who are already exhausted *before* a big presentation, after adrenaline and anxiety have robbed them of sleep and sapped their energy reserves over preceding days.)

These energy reserves were important on this occasion as the curse seemed like it would continue - Geelong were leading by 19 points midway through the final quarter, but Hawthorn rallied and won by 5 points. The curse was vanquished.

The following week the Hawks won the 2013 Grand Final by defeating Fremantle. (In 2014 and 2015, they won again in a rare three-in-a-row performance).

Do game-day messages tip the scales to victory?

We can't know exactly how influential these messages are, but we know they are important. Many great wins are linked to powerful messages driving the teams, and many players remember them as important. For example, in 2013 the players used the following words when remembering the white line presentation:

"It stood out, we wondered what he was doing, it was really powerful."

"It sent shivers up the spine."

"I reckon all of the boys would have remembered, as soon as they stepped onto the MCG and over that white line, exactly what Clarko spoke about."

THE POWER OF MESSAGING IN 4 AREAS OF LIFE...

Messaging can help you too. You might want to change the world, or perhaps just part of your own world. Messaging...

1. Makes great leaders.

2. Gets your ideas heard.

3. Builds your personal brand.

4. Promotes your organisation.

These 4 areas include examples from people I've worked with as well as some successful people who have inspired me (and millions of others).

MESSAGING MAKES GREAT LEADERS

Great leaders are always associated with memorable messages. This is no coincidence. It's the impact of their messages that determines whether they are seen as great leaders. If you are a leader, *your messages are the reason people follow you*. Your reputation consists of either the messages you drive home or the messages other people pass on about you. Here are some examples ...

Gandhi - Spreading a new idea

Mohandas Gandhi changed the world with his 'non-violent, non-cooperation' position against the British occupation of India.

He is considered the father of the Indian independence movement. Gandhi's leadership success actually began in South Africa, where he lived for 20 years. It was there he refined his concept of non-violent protesting against injustices.

A British-educated Barrister, Gandhi had a pivotal life experience just a week after he arrived in 1893, when, as a first class passenger, he was famously thrown off a train at Pietermaritzburg simply for being Indian. Rather than retaliate or take the insult personally, his experience led him to test his leadership ideas.

Later, when he returned to India, Gandhi assumed the leadership of the Indian National Congress. He led nationwide campaigns for easing poverty, expanding women's rights, ending untouchability, but above all for achieving Indian self-rule.

Many civil rights leaders, including Martin Luther King and Nelson Mandela, used Gandhi's concept of non-violent protest as a model for their own struggles. Here are his top 3 leadership messages.

"In this cause, I am prepared to die, but there is no cause for which I am prepared to kill."

This leadership message was so memorable that it was forever captured in the Richard Attenborough film, *Gandhi*. It was on September 11, 1906, that Gandhi addressed a group of 3,000 Indians in Johannesburg.

The group was angry towards the discriminative laws against the colony's Indian population. Just minutes before his brilliant message was delivered, many in the audience were advocating violence. One person jumped up and exclaimed, "I am willing to die to fight these laws". Then Gandhi delivered the message that both composed and inspired the group.

"In this cause, I too am prepared to die, but there is no cause for which I am prepared to kill."

The room went into a shocked silence with the power of this idea. It's worth remembering that Gandhi was not known as a charismatic speaker. He just delivered his leadership messages and let them sink into people's minds. His leadership ideas had all the power required to change people's thinking.

With this statement, Gandhi was able to short circuit the anger in the room, yet satisfy the desire for action. And, by the end of the speech he had them agree to take an oath to both resist the unjust laws, yet without violence.

This is leadership at it's most potent. He led the group with the clarity of his idea. His message was so vivid, and so transferable that he crystallised the non-violent, non-cooperation movement for the rest of the world to use.

"Be the change you wish to see in the world."

This is probably Gandhi's most famous quote. You may have heard it before but not realised it came from Gandhi. It's been repeated by so many people now this leadership idea has a life of its own. It's an example of a leadership message continuing to lead, long after the man is gone.

Gandhi came across a lot of people who had dogmatic views about how other people should act and what they should do. This message confronts the lack of thinking associated with dogma and turns it around to ask, 'what are you doing with your life and the everyday moments you have?'

The famous Gandhi sugar story

A woman walks with her son many miles to see Gandhi. She is worried her son is eating too much sugar. She asks Gandhi: "Please, sir, can you tell my son to stop eating sugar."

Gandhi says, "Bring him back in 2 weeks." Disappointed, she takes her son home.

Two weeks later she makes the long journey again. Gandhi says to the boy, "you must stop eating sugar. It's very bad for you." The boy has such respect for Gandhi that he stops and lives a healthy life.

The woman is confused and asks, "Why did you want me to wait 2 weeks to bring back my son."

Gandhi said, "Because before I could tell your son to stop eating sugar, *I* had to stop eating sugar."

The leadership idea: Changing yourself might help more than telling others they have to change. Further still, he said that by changing yourself, you will change how you feel and what actions you take. And so have a tangible impact on the world around you.

**"I want to change their minds. Not kill them
for weaknesses we all possess."**

Boom! Another leadership message home-run.

When faced with a group of Indian political leaders who wanted to go to war with the British, Gandhi was able to change the minds of the people in the room by doing 2 things:

1) Focusing on the similarities we have with others, even our enemies.
2) Reminding everyone of their goal: To change the minds of the British leadership and get them to leave India.

This leadership message dissolved their violent rage. In just 5 seconds. When we realise we're all imperfect it becomes easier to see alternative ways of connecting with people who are, after all, just people. (You may recall that another of Gandhi's messages along these lines is *An eye for an eye makes the whole world blind*'.)

For many years, Indian politicians would seek the advice of Gandhi before making key decisions. On this occasion in Congress in September 1920, politicians were poised to use violence to fight the British for independence.

Through his messages, Gandhi was able to convince the leaders to focus their efforts on the non-violent, non-cooperation movement, which ultimately led to the withdrawal of the British from India in 1947 – and set a precedent that may last for centuries.

Gandhi's Leadership Ideas

Gandhi's leadership ideas had a profound impact on the world. Albert Einstein captured this impact when he said: *"Generations to come, it may well be, will scarce believe that such a man as this one ever in flesh and blood walked upon this Earth."*

Nelson Mandela – His life in messages

It makes sense to talk about Mandela next, because Gandhi's messages had a profound impact on Mandela. A message that has the power to be *transferred* from one person to another, is a message that has a life of its own. This kind of *transferable message* is the holy grail of communication.

Nelson Mandela's leadership example started with angry protest, but he grew into a humble, eloquent and inspirational figure who advocated peace, democracy and human rights.

After being in jail for 29 years as a political prisoner, he was released in 1990, joined negotiations to abolish apartheid and to establish multi-racial elections, and was elected President of South Africa in 1994.

Nelson Mandela was an incredibly effective leader. Here are some of his leadership messages that mobilised a movement and made him an inspiration to millions.

"I learned that courage was not the absence of fear, but the triumph over it."

Mandela continued: "The brave man is not he who does not feel afraid, but he who conquers that fear."

Why is this message so powerful? Because he was asking people to join him in a fight against those with the guns and all the power. He knew they were scared. He used this message to seek support for his cause (even from jail). He gave them this inspirational message: if you're afraid; it's normal, you're still a brave person. What you need to do next is to conquer that fear by taking action.

This line is the result of a powerful technique for persuasion. I call it the "You may be thinking…" technique. By anticipating an audience's questions, you address the concern or question in their mind. You then go past this question to the answer.

This connects with people on a deep level. Firstly, it builds trust because people see that you understand their view. And secondly it clears the objection and makes new space in their mind for your message.

"No one is born hating another person because of the colour of his skin, or his background, or his religion."

He continues: "People must learn to hate, and if they can learn to hate, they can be taught to love, for love comes more naturally to the human heart than its opposite."

When you think about it, this makes sense. This leadership message shakes up our thinking and gives us a fresh way to view a situation.

This is a long message, more like an explanation, but it says so much. Like all great leaders, Nelson Mandela was able to change the viewpoint of his listeners in just a few words.

"Resentment is like drinking poison and then hoping it will kill your enemies."

Boom. It says so much in so few words.

Here he asks people not to retaliate with violence after they win their struggle. Nelson Mandela was inspired by Gandhi's leadership example of non-violent change. When Mandela was elected President of South Africa in 1994 he encouraged his supporters to forgive their former oppressors, rather than fight back with violence.

Why? It wasn't only about doing the 'right thing'. With this brilliant, short yet powerful message, he showed that resentment and retribution won't help them.

He said: *'Don't get even, don't pay them back because it won't help you. It won't make you feel better. It won't help you build a better society for your children. It will only corrupt you'.*

What followed was 3 years of transformation, reconciliation and forgiveness that finally ended apartheid in South Africa. During this time, another message Nelson Mandela shared was, *"If you want to make peace with your enemy, you have to work with your enemy. Then he becomes your partner."*

Not only does this message guide us in the right direction, it just makes sense. And that's why we trust the leader.

Nelson Mandela is a global leadership example. Not only did he lead South Africa through massive challenges, he set an example of inspirational leadership that continues to inspire and motivate. It's a wonderful legacy.

Steve Jobs - Chief Messaging Officer

Steve Jobs changed the world in a different way. He redefined how we interact with and use technology. And messaging was his secret weapon. Here's how Steve Jobs changed the world in the following areas:

- **Computers**. He co-founded Apple Computer and led the team that created the Macintosh in 1984, the first computer with a graphical user interface and mouse.
- **Music**. He created the iPod and iTunes Store, which changed the way people purchase and access music.
- **Consumer technology**. The iPhone and iPad are full-powered pocket computers that launched the 'post-PC era', in which

personal computer sales declined and consumer devices - that are portable, always connected and have access to cloud-based services - are the growing trend.

- **Pixar.** In his spare time he created Pixar, which changed the world of animated movies.

Chief Messaging Officer

What's unique about Steve Jobs is his *direct involvement* in the messaging of his industry, his company and the specific products he launched. It was highly unusual that a CEO (as opposed to an advertising agency) would decide on messaging, let alone launch each product personally to deliver those messages.

For example, leading up to the iPod launch in October 2001, Steve personally managed the process of deciding on both the name and the message of this breakthrough product. What's interesting is that Steve decided on the message *before* they had named the product. The message – '1000 songs in your pocket' – was clear in his mind some months before the name 'iPod' was chosen.

Let's look at this example of messaging and how it helped the iPod garner an 80% share of the MP3 music player market and set Apple on a trajectory to become the most valuable company in the world.

The master of the transferable message

When Jobs walked on stage on October 23, 2001, to launch the iPod, he began by talking about how much he and people at Apple loved music. He went on to lament the fact that the current crop of MP3 players were frustrating and, in many cases, unusable.

Then he started talking about what would make a great MP3 player; this included storing a lot of songs – say, 1000 songs – so you wouldn't have to keep syncing it with your computer. It would have to be small enough to fit in your pocket, he said. Plus, it should have a user interface that makes it quick and easy to find the song you want.

Then he paused and said, "Well, I have this perfect product right here in my pocket."

He pulled it out of his front jeans pocket and said,

"The iPod. 1000 songs in your pocket."

At the same moment, the screen behind him reinforced the message like a billboard. Within an hour, the Apple homepage was emblazoned with the same message. 'The iPod. 1000 songs in your pocket'. It was very clear.

Smart messaging gets massive editorial exposure for free!

With his vivid language, Steve Jobs achieved what other leaders have only dreamed of; massive editorial exposure for free.

How? The audience was filled with hundreds of journalists and reviewers who wrote articles about the iPod and, of course, included the *'1000 songs in your pocket'* message as either a **headline** or a key component of the **first couple of paragraphs**.

In fact, the transferable-message-genius of Steve Jobs went further than that. Purchasers of the iPod proudly showed it to their friends, dutifully repeating the message. *"Hey, have you seen this? 1000 songs in your pocket!"*

Steve achieved the same messaging magic with most of his product launches. For example, he very cleverly set up the iPhone presentation with the promise that he was launching **"3 revolutionary products**.
- A widescreen iPod with touch controls
- A revolutionary mobile phone
- A breakthrough internet communications device".

He spoke about these 3 products for a while, toying with his audience for a few minutes. Then, delivered the vivid message:

"These are not 3 separate devices. This is 1 device.
And we're calling it iPhone."

Guess which message was repeated by thousands of journalists and reviewers that day?

"The new iPhone is 3 products in 1."

You can leverage the power of messaging

Steve Jobs had other skills you and I may not be able to easily replicate – like his hypnotic charisma, stubbornness and intense focus – but we can all leverage the power of messaging. Here are some messages he used to build his success:

"You can change the world."

When Steve Jobs was a kid, he saw a new piece of technology – a speaker that didn't need an amplifier. He went home and told his dad, who said, "Every speaker needs an amplifier, son". He forced his dad to come with him to look at the new technology, and observed his dad's amazement. Steve credits this moment as the start of a driving belief that he had for the rest of his life:

'The people who created all the stuff in the world are no smarter than you or me.'

So he decided that it was quite logical and possible that he would change the world. He's also known for convincing many brilliant people to work for him on the promise that they could, literally, change the world. Most famously, when Steve Jobs enticed the CEO of Pepsi to become Apple CEO in its early days. The message that finally convinced John Scully to quit his safe job at Pepsi and join the risky young Apple team was:

"Do you want to sell sugar water for the rest of your life, or do you want to change the world?"

John Scully says this is what persuaded him to join Apple.

Here's an unconventional message:

"This is shit!"

Jobs was a great motivator, but a hard man to work for at times. He expected perfection – sometimes an impossible perfection – from his engineers. He was famous for giving a *'This is shit'* response to the first look at software and hardware prototypes.

Now, you might be wondering if this is, in fact, a motivating leadership message to his team! However, his team worked out that "This is shit" actually meant; "Why is this the best way to do it?"

This ultimately forced people to think through their projects and make sure it was the best option. It helped create a culture that was focused on making insanely great products.

Changing the framework of a discussion

Jobs also used messaging to dissolve problems. The 'Antennagate' crisis happened soon after the launch of the iPhone 4 in July 2010.

The iPhone 4 was a great smartphone, but it used a design where the antenna was wrapped around the outside edge of the phone. If you held it in a certain way, a finger would bridge the gap between 2 antenna segments and the signal was weakened.

It became known as the 'death grip' and in some cases might even cause a dropped call. There was a huge media outcry with calls for a worldwide product recall.

Steve Jobs rushed back from his family Hawaiian vacation to address the negative perceptions. He held a media presentation that changed the framework of the discussion. He led with a message that surprised many people. Rather than apologising, he said, 'Phones aren't perfect' and proceeded to explain why it's not a big problem.

"We're not perfect. Phones are not perfect. We all know that. But we want to make our customers happy."

This is a great example of a leadership message. He decided that the way people were viewing the problem was wrong – and he gave them another view. That's leadership.

Some people said it was more like bullshit than leadership. However people's anger and frustration dissolved. And to top his message off, he said, "…but we want to make you happy so here's a free plastic 'bumper' that solves the problem". He offered that to anyone who wanted one. His message changed the conversation in 4 short sentences.

The most watched speech in the world

"Stay hungry. Stay Foolish."

This message took on a life of its own after Steve Jobs made a low-key speech at Stanford University in 2005, that later went viral on the internet. Over 50,000,000 people have watched it. Most heard about it through word of mouth.

The full speech was later published in *Fortune* magazine. Now, I've been reading Fortune for over 20 years and never before or after, have they published a speech. This speech made an impact.

Why was this speech so good? It contains a *life leadership* message. It was written for a stadium full of 20-somethings who were graduating university and starting their working lives (it turns out that many millions more needed to hear this message too).

The speech covers the fascinating story of Steve Jobs' life building Apple Computer and Pixar Animation Studios, as well as a discussion of the meaning of life and death. Everything he talks about in the speech reinforces, and leads to, his powerful take-home message.

The 'Stay hungry. Stay foolish' message is short and simple. However it encapsulates the ideas reflected throughout the speech. Here are some of the other points within the speech that support and reinforce his shorter message:

"The only way to do great work is love what you do. If you haven't found it, keep looking. Don't settle."

"When I was 17, I read a quote that went something like: 'If you live each day like it's your last, someday you'll most certainly be right.' It made an impression on me, and ever since then, for the last 33 years, I have looked in the mirror every morning and asked myself: 'If today were the last day of my life, would I want to do what I am about to do today?' And whenever the answer has been 'No' for too many days in a row, I know I need to change something."

"Your time is limited, don't waste it living someone else's life. Don't be trapped by dogma, which is living the result of other people's thinking."

"Don't let the noise of other opinions drown your own inner voice. And most important, have the courage to follow your heart and intuition, they somehow already know what you truly want to become. Everything else is secondary."

So…his message for your life is:

"Stay hungry. Stay foolish."

(By the way, guess which headline the *Fortune* editors chose when they published the speech?)

David Morrison, Army Chief - Changing the culture

In 2013, the leader of the Australian Army had to deal with a crisis. In the midst of another sex scandal, around a 'Jedi Council' internet sex ring, a leadership speech delivered by Chief of the Army, Lieutenant-General David Morrison, was posted as a 3 minute video.

The speech is good. However, people forget most of what they hear no matter how good a speech is. It's the catchy message that has the most impact. His leadership message:

"The standard you walk past is the standard you accept."

This message has now worked it's way into leadership conversations all around the world. Here are 3 reasons why it works so well:

1. It makes every listener responsible for leadership

This message forces people to see that *their* actions make a difference to the culture of the organisation. Morrison said:

"Every one of us is responsible for the culture and reputation

of our army and the environment in which we work. If you become aware of any individual degrading another, then show moral courage and take a stand against it." "If that does not suit you then get out."

2. The message is unmistakeable

It's the nature of the human mind that listeners will forget most of what the speaker says. That's why *message recall* is so important. I spoke to dozens of people about this speech and asked them what they thought the key message was. They all nominated *'The standard you walk past is the standard you accept'*.

Admittedly, they couldn't all repeat the message word for word, some people repeated it as: 'If you walk past something, you're accepting it' or 'You have to set the standard and not walk past it' or 'There was a great line from that speech! Something about standards... Help me remember, um...' But when they were reminded of it, they showed instant recognition. Not 100% recollection perhaps, but recall on most leadership speeches is zero.

3. His delivery is aligned with the message

Delivery skills *follow* the clarity of your message. They flow naturally when the message is clear in your mind and therefore, clearly reflected in your words. Each speaker should be involved in crafting their own messages to help their natural delivery skills magic to work.

In this speech, Morrison shows genuine emotion. We see his pain and we are sure he means what he says. His delivery is slow enough to emphasise what's important. He seems like it's *his* message, not something he said because his PR team told him he had to make a speech.

He comes across as a leader because he shows how he cares about his organisation. It's a serious tone, but it is seen as a caring tone as well because he cares for the people in his team and wants them to thrive in his organisation.

CEO - The reason for the new plan

Change is always resisted. And most organisational initiatives fail to live up to their potential as a result. So, a good leader explains *why* things are changing.

The CEO of a large entertainment company asked my opinion on his new *Company Values* initiative being rolled out. I said, 'The values look fine, but what's your message?'

He said, "What do you mean? There's no message. These are the values. My leadership team has agreed on them. We will explain them to our senior managers and they will pass them on to the rest of the team. Simple. Why are you always going on about the message, Cam?"

"Ok, how long has it been since the last 'Company Values' rollout? It might have been called a corporate purpose, vision, mission statement or corporate philosophy", I asked.

"Oh, about 18 months."

"What about the one before that?" I asked.

Pause... "About 2 years before that" he responded.

I asked if any of his direct reports had been in the company for 5 years or more, and had therefore experienced 2 similar rollouts.

His eyes widened as he said, "Yes, most of them".

"So, is it possible that some of the smart ones will be thinking, 'I wonder how long these 'Values' will last before the *next* rollout?' Is it possible that a number of your broader team will smile and nod to your rollout, but think that the smart move would be not to invest too much effort into this version?"

His head dropped briefly, before he sat up tall and said, "You're right. That's exactly what they'll be thinking!".

Leaders are often so close to an issue, they fail to remember that staff have not experienced the full debate and may not be clear on the 'reasons why'. There is usually a need for a message to position a new initiative.

The 'values' versus the 'values message'

A new initiative is a bit like a new house that staff are told they must now live in, while the message addresses (no pun intended) *why* they need a new house. The message deals with the natural resistance to the effort and uncertainty of the move.

So, before our conversation, the message to launch the new 'Values' was essentially:

> *'We are all going to work with these 6 values from now on. Here they are... (the 6 values were listed and examples provided).'*

After we identified the unanswered questions in the minds of the audience and recognised the resistance they would create, we came up with this message:

> *'Here are the new values. You might be wondering what happened to the last set of values. Good question. They were okay, however the organisation is changing for the better and these new values underpin the change. Living these values is a better way to work because we'll all have more freedom to try things – that is, you'll have more support, which should make work more enjoyable and satisfying.'*

This message guides the presentations and other conversations needed to ensure the change initiative 'sticks'. And it provides clear direction for anyone attempting to talk about the issue.

The weakest link

The message supporting an initiative is often the weakest link in the chain when attempting culture change or behaviour change. Getting this message right breaks down obstacles to acceptance and creates momentum.

MESSAGING GETS YOUR IDEAS HEARD

Anita Roddick - Media exposure for free

Great entrepreneurs are usually great at crafting vivid messages. Messages that live in our minds and are passed onto others.

Founder of The Body Shop, Anita Roddick, is a prime example of achieving prolific success through communication skills. Anita founded the Body Shop brand with just 1 store in 1976 and grew it to 2,000 stores. For most of their high growth years, The Body Shop didn't spend a single cent on advertising.

Yes, you read that correctly!

Anita saw opportunities to promote her messages everywhere – including staff T-shirts, shop windows, walls and even delivery trucks.

She grew The Body Shop by rejecting conventional marketing. She crafted memorable slogans and made bold public pronouncements that manifested a brand identity.

The last time I saw her speak at a leadership event in Sydney (along with Jack Welch, Bill Clinton and Tom Peters), she was introduced by best-selling author Marcus Buckingham with, "I don't think there's any more extraordinary human being on earth than Anita Roddick. You know when they use the term 'walk the talk'? She invented the term walk the talk".

How to get Massive Media Exposure without Advertising

Anita Roddick had an amazing ability get her ideas heard. Even her consumers became marketers as they shared ideas and leaflets. She liked to be provocative and took strong positions on issues. For example:

"**Educate rather than create hype.**"

The Body Shop got a lot of publicity through their social activism. They stood for something – and got press attention as a result. For example, Anita Roddick was a vocal opponent of animal testing, and that crusade became one of her biggest calling cards.

As a result of her unconventional stand on world issues, The Body Shop got an enormous amount of attention from the press.

'Ruby' Barbie Doll

Another memorable example was their unconventional take on their Barbie doll dubbed 'Ruby'. The campaign featured a doll with a large, curvy figure with the slogan;

"There are 3 billion women who don't look like supermodels and only 8 who do."

The image was posted on Body Shop windows across the world and challenged people to think differently about existing stereotypes of beauty.

Anita's Ruby campaign in 1997 kick-started a worldwide debate on body image and self-esteem. People discussed it and the media talked about it.

This is the holy grail of communication: transferable messages!

It's amazing to think that Anita Roddick was nominated for UK Marketing Hall of Fame, even though The Body Shop didn't run advertising campaigns.

Anita Roddick's business vision was founded on being different. Business was a means to drive social and environmental change, as well as make a dollar. Her messaging created financial success as well. The Body Shop was sold to L'Oréal for almost $1 billion in 2006 and Anita pocketed $200 million. Her message about business was:

"Find new ways to push the limits of business and make it a force for positive change."

She said, "Knowledge, unless it goes through the heart, is dangerous". It was through her genius as a communicator that Anita Roddick was able to inspire people, create change and give people things to believe in.

Her 'key to leadership', however, is my favourite. She said:

"Leadership *is* communication."

She said that the most important tool you've got as a leader is communication.

"Make it bold and enlivening and passionate – if you can't communicate, you're just not there."

Another technique she used was repetition. That's right, repetition.

You've got to keep talking, and keep on communicating your message over and over – and over! I remember her take home message from that leadership session in Sydney:

"When you are exhausted from repeating yourself, and you think everybody else is exhausted from hearing – repeat it again! You're probably just starting to get your message across".

If you read her great autobiography 'Business as Unusual', you'll notice that nearly every page has a message in bold, double sized text to illuminate the big ideas from the detail.

Allan Carr - The EasyWay to stop smoking

In a world of gum, patches and other ingenious nicotine delivery methods, 'The EasyWay to stop smoking' is considered the most successful method to quit. It's amazing. And it's built simply on a vivid message and supporting explanations, via his book or seminars. The EasyWay book has sold 13 million copies and has many raving fans, including:

> *"It was such a revelation that instantly I was freed from my addiction." - Sir Anthony Hopkins*

> *"Everybody who reads the book quits." - Ellen DeGeneres*

> *"At the end of the book you take your last smoke and you're done. I haven't smoked since." - Ashton Kutcher*

> *"His method removes your dependence while you smoke. It worked for me." - Sir Richard Branson*

Allen Carr quit smoking after 33 years as a 100-a-day chain smoker. He claims that 2 key pieces of information crystallised in his mind just how easy it was to stop.

First, a hypnotherapist told him smoking was 'just nicotine addiction' which Allen had never perceived before. Second, his son John lent him a medical handbook which explained that the physical withdrawal from nicotine is just like an 'empty, insecure feeling'.

From there, he isolated a message:

"Smoking doesn't relax you, smoking creates an ongoing agitation that can only be relieved by having a cigarette."

The smoker had an existing belief: smoking is relaxing. And they needed to relax in this stressful world, so giving up smoking was just too difficult. So, the message the smoker had in their mind as they lifted their arm and placed the cigarette between their lips, was:

"Smoking a cigarette will relax me."

If you're going to change the way people think, you have to understand the beliefs or messages they already carry in their mind. Allen Carr understood this and developed a method that was able to *replace the existing message* in the mind of the smoker.

In fact, as you read his book, or progress through his seminar, you are asked to periodically have a cigarette. So the new ideas are linked with the current behaviour. At the end of the book or session, you take your final smoke, but it's now *associated with a new message*. As you lift your arm and place the cigarette between your lips, the message now is:

"Smoking a cigarette will create agitation."

Of course, he needed more than just a message. He needed explanations, analogies, stories and examples. So he wrote a book and developed a 3-hour session which reinforced his message. These sessions are delivered by 100s of psychologists around the world to guide people out of the maze of smoking addiction.

Within his book and his courses, he dispels myths and uses the following **explanations** for his message:

Myth 1. Smokers need willpower to quit: He explains that, contrary to their perception, smokers do not receive a boost from smoking: it only relieves the withdrawal symptoms from the *previous* cigarette, which in turn creates more withdrawal symptoms once it is finished. He explains that the 'relief' smokers feel on lighting a cigarette, the feeling of being 'back to normal', is the feeling experienced by non-smokers all the time.

Myth 2. Smokers choose to smoke: He explains that after the experimental cigarettes it's the nicotine addiction that traps you. If you've ever once tried to stop smoking, you realise it's not a choice to continue.

Myth 3. Smokers will suffer terrible physical nicotine withdrawal if they quit: He argues that withdrawal is minor, but the **belief** that you'll suffer is the main cause of the pain and frustration. The withdrawal symptoms are actually created by doubt and fear (uncertainty), and therefore that stopping smoking is not as traumatic as is commonly assumed, *if* that doubt and fear can be removed.

With these explanations, people understand his core message that 'smoking a cigarette will create agitation', and they just stop! The message is embedded in their brain and drives their new-found positive behaviour.

Steve Waugh - Leadership for a new audience

Steve Waugh is a legendary cricketer who captained the Australian Cricket Team from 1999 – 2004. He has shown great leadership off the field as well, particularly in philanthropy and publishing. He's written 13 books.

I worked with Steve recently, helping to structure his leadership ideas for a full-day corporate event.

It's one thing for a leader to respond instinctively and execute leadership wisdom in their chosen field. It's another thing to repackage that wisdom for a business audience and deliver it from the stage in bite-sized chunks.

To share his knowledge, he first had to isolate the messages and examples his audience could relate to. *This* is the skill that makes you a great speaker. *What's the point of the story? What's the learning from the event? What's the message from the coaching session?* This is what audiences crave.

When he first sat down to prepare for the event, he found it difficult to know where to start. However, after isolating his messages, it was wonderful to see Steve easily access a range of examples to support each point.

From his sporting success, to breaking new ground in publishing, to a whole range of philanthropic events and organisations in Australia, Europe and the Subcontinent. Steve seems to be living many lives.

Here are some of his key messages and the examples that flowed from them:

"Assume nothing."

"Winning leads to complacency. It's just human nature. It can be a trap. You can't rely on past success and so you must go forward facing the truth head-on. What I mean

by this is that sometimes it's necessary to make hard or unpopular decisions that ultimately benefit the team (or the organisation). Even when these truths are things that you don't want to hear, that you don't want to believe. Like cutting a popular player from the next Test series. Assuming nothing also means that you don't have to continue to follow a path or direction that's no longer working. It's never too late to review and refocus."

"If I'm going to make a mistake, it will be an original one, not somebody else's."

"A leader ultimately has to trust his gut and have a personal vision for the success of the team. This involves going out on a limb, but it's something a leader must do. You should expect to make mistakes, but at least if they're your mistakes you'll learn from them.

Early on as captain of the Australian Cricket team, I followed the advice of the team manager. It turned out to be a mistake. Of course, everybody makes mistakes, but I thought at the time; 'How dumb was that! Not only was it a mistake, but it wasn't my judgment, so I didn't learn the lesson and integrate that into my thinking.'

Another example is in publishing. My most recent book was self-published. A lot of people said it was a mistake but we looked at it closely and took the risk. That book, The Meaning of Luck, retailed for half the price of similar books, sold a huge number of copies and made a greater profit than if we'd signed to a publisher. The decision could quite easily have been a mistake, but the end-result was a great success."

"Why can't we win every game?"

"I'm a big believer in having realistic leadership expectations. If people don't believe the goal is achievable, then energy dissipates. In fact, personally, as a batsman, I would set the smallest goal to ensure I was focused on the ball in front of

me. For example, in my first game for Australia, my goal was not to get 100, it was simply 'don't get a duck'. That was the goal. It was a realistic expectation to build from.

*But a leader also **sets the vision**, and one day, after looking at our form I posed the question to the team: 'Why can't we win every game on this tour?*

Let's think about this for a minute. Here's how good we are, here's our strategy and here's our opposition. Why can't we win every game?' And we did. This question crystallised in every player's mind that it was possible. It focused us on achieving a previously unheard of goal. And it led to a World record of 16 consecutive Test victories."

"Don't get bitter, get better."

"You get better results when you focus your energies correctly. You don't want to waste energy on things that don't move you or the team forward. I'm competitive and have a drive to beat the other team, but when I see people getting bitter or angry, I always ask whether it's focused energy or wasted energy.

So in cricket, when frustrating things happened or when there was heated rivalry between teams, I liked to refocus the team on getting better (not bitter)."

Politician - How much water to grow an orange?

There has been plenty of debate in desert-filled Australia about the best use of water. There are regular arguments between farmers, politicians and environmentalist about the diverting of water from rivers, like the Murray, to grow fruit.

This debate has been heated and aggressive and often included the fact that much of our produce was exported to other countries. One day, a simple message was thrown into the debate that changed everyone's perspective.

'When we export fruit, we are exporting water.'

This message quickly prompted questions like: What is the physical cost of the water? What is the opportunity cost of the water? What price are we getting for our water in exports?

This led to a much more balanced debate.

Doctor - Convincing people to support a new idea

Ok. Vagina. There, I've said it. It made me feel awkward, but it needed to be said to outline an example of one doctor's attempt to convince surgeons to change their behaviour.

A few years ago, I worked with Dr Marcus Carey, a Melbourne-based uro-gynaecologist to help him 'sell' a new idea. He had developed a groundbreaking medical procedure to treat vaginal prolapse and he needed to refine his persuasive skills so he could change the behaviours of surgeons around the world.

Working with Johnson and Johnson, Dr Carey had developed a new operation but still had to personally convince people to change what they were currently doing.

Great ideas do not always sell themselves. This doctor was doing what all leaders have to do – persuade people to change their thinking. However, people resist change because it involves effort and uncertainty.

Even great ideas can fail without persuasion

Someone has to get the word out to convince people to change behaviour. Dr Carey had the right idea; he was scheduled to speak at medical conferences around the world.

And there is a global need for his idea. Consider: The current operation required tremendous skill by the surgeon and there weren't enough trained surgeons to meet the demand. The current operation took 3 hours, versus less than 1 hour for the new one. With an ageing population, there is a 45% increase in the demand for prolapse surgery. 1 in 8 women experience a variation of this condition.

Dr Carey's surgical procedure was more effective in a number of ways. But his initial explanation was way too long and technical. We refined the message to:

"This new operation has 4 benefits over the existing method:

1, it's quicker – reducing surgical risk,

2, it's less aggressive – providing faster healing,

3, it reduces the chances of later complications, and, it's much easier to explain to patients."

His earlier communications included many of these points, but they were lost in the details. After we defined his 4-point message, he had a flexible, memorable and transferable summary, that could be conveyed in less than 20 seconds. The fact that it's short makes it more likely that people will repeat it.

So, this story is about an idea/technique/procedure that is much better than the existing one. If you want your ideas heard, you can learn from this example. Unfortunately, many great ideas do fail because they're not communicated well enough to convince people.

MESSAGING BUILDS YOUR PERSONAL BRAND

Packaging your knowledge into *messages, presentations* or *focused conversations* helps build your personal brand and increases the value of your ideas.

Jules Lund - Finding the message changed everything, effortlessly

---

Jules Lund was already a well-known TV and radio presenter when we met a couple of years ago. However, he was a little anxious about his upcoming speech to 1,000 people at the Australian Radio Conference. He hadn't done many 'business presentations' like this. And he wanted to use this opportunity to brand himself as an expert on social media.

Jules asked me a range of questions; what's the best way to structure his ideas? How much detail to include? What are the best delivery techniques to engage the audience? Etc.

However, one simple thing we did at the start of our session answered all those questions *automatically*. We changed the title from;

'*How to leverage Social Media*'

to,

'*Your Digital Portfolio*'.

Why did that make such a difference?

His first title seemed accurate and informative, but it positioned him on the same footing as 100 other experts on social media. And he was missing an opportunity. Because, after chatting with Jules it became clear that he was not just saying 'you need to be good at social media and here's how to do it', he was saying that social media is *as important* as your radio show. So we changed the title to 'Your digital portfolio'.

Radio stations now have a 'digital portfolio'

In other words, the radio network with the studios, expensive radio licence and the broadcasting tower on top of the hill - the thing assumed to have the most value - was only *1* part of their business now. They needed to stop thinking of having a radio station and then adding some social media. They needed to focus their resources differently, because, they were now an entertainment company that had a 'digital portfolio' that included 3 things:

1. Their existing radio station

2. Their website

3. Their social media audience.

All 3 were now **equal** in value and importance. This was a dramatic shattering of radio management's current perception. And a difficult one to face up to for Jules' audience. It ultimately meant big balance-sheet write-downs of the value of a radio licence.

This change occurred so quickly that no-one had really seen it this way.

Jules' presentation explaining this change (and what to do about it) blew the audience away. It convinced owners and managers of the largest networks in Australia and Asia to rethink their strategy and their resource allocation based on this new view of a digital portfolio. And it positioned Jules as a *thought leader* in entertainment.

How can changing a title make such a difference?

Why did changing the title (and the ultimate message) change all the other important elements of a speech or presentation? Three reasons.

Firstly, clarity. We changed the title because we had found the real message. This gave Jules laser-like focus, making it clear what details to include and what was no longer needed in his presentation. The structuring of his ideas was now easy. For example, as we went through the chunk structure, Jules could see that 20 slides on how social media works were no longer necessary.

Secondly, energy. The excitement Jules had for the presentation once the message was clear was amazing to see. His posture changed. From weighed down by a busy schedule, trying to find time to put a great presentation together in his spare hours, to absolute certainty he had a valuable message to share with his industry.

Thirdly, delivery. The clarity and energy that was manifest *effortlessly* from finding the real message, was evident in every word and move Jules made while delivering the presentation. Anxiety and uncertainty dissolved as his clarity and certainty took over.

His presentation was fantastic. The audience raved. And Jules Lund built a profitable and influential brand as an expert.

Janine Allis - Messaging allows natural style

The wildly successful marketing of Boost Juice is synonymous with its founder, Janine Allis. Janine is a genius at promoting herself and her business, which means she is a genius at delivering memorable messages. Her key branding message is an oft-repeated story.

> *'A mom with 3 kids, who left school at 16, started Boost Juice in her family kitchen, and has grown to 200 stores.'*

This is the sort of message that gets passed on at dinner parties and in general conversation. For example, at the shopping centre, *"Let's get a Boost Juice. Hey, did you know the woman who started it left school at 16?"*

One of the memorable things about Janine's story is that her formal qualifications from Knox Technical School didn't include Business Administration, they included typing and welding! How do I know this? Because Janine has repeated the 'typing and welding' story in support of her core message many times. It's part of Boost Juice folklore.

'Solving problems and keeping things simple'

Janine is also very good at 'speaking in messages' to the media. For example, when asked 'How did you grow such a successful business with little schooling and no formal training Janine?'

"I'm not good at everything, but what I am good at is solving problems and keeping things simple."

Great. 'Solving problems and keeping things simple'. That's the kind of message that will make a magazine headline. And it did! By speaking in messages, you have greater control of your brand.

I had the pleasure of working with Janine as her early success led to public speaking opportunities. As she became more famous and the audiences got bigger, she found it a challenge to relax and be herself on stage. For example, Janine didn't like to wear suits, but needed to speak to 500 people dressed in suits.

She had questions about her brand, her natural style and what these new audiences expected. As long as these questions remained unresolved they created uncertainty, and uncertainty saps energy levels and feeds anxiety when speaking.

Should I follow a script?

She wondered: Should I follow a script? Should I change my style and my approach for different audiences? And, if I do, how much? *And* if I do that, will I lose myself and my ability to think clearly and speak naturally when attempting to satisfy these varied audiences?

All normal and important questions in this situation.

One of the specific challenges Janine had in grappling with these questions was that she didn't like to follow a script, however, she would often get lost as she went off on (interesting) tangents. This made her feel uncomfortable and uncertain about how to get back on track during a speech.

For someone who was very good at controlling her environment, with a beautifully practical mind, Janine found the uncertainty unpleasant and wanted to improve.

We talked about the fact that people loved her unconventional approach and natural style. It was Janine's genuineness, even with rough edges, that attracted people to her story.

She said, 'Great! I don't want to change my style. But how can I master public speaking?'

The question now was; How could Janine create an environment where she felt comfortable on stage - no matter how large the audience? Following a script was not the answer. Rarely does following a script help a speaker connect to an audience.

The answer was to identify key messages for her stories, so even if she went off on a tangent or went a bit longer on a story, she knew how to end each story.

The messages were her anchors throughout a speech, presentation or media interview. This approach worked beautifully. It reduced her uncertainty, renewed her energy levels and dissolved the anxiety associated with larger presentations.

Raw and unpolished but able to capture an audience

In his 2005 biography of Janine called *Business secrets of the woman behind Boost Juice*, business journalist James Kirby described her public speaking as 'raw and unpolished but able to capture the audience with her natural style'.

Brilliant. The word unpolished is now a compliment! It's clarity around key messages that allows her to relax and speak naturally. Janine Allis has now told her story to hundreds of thousands of people at events all over the world, and it has helped drive Boost Juice's success.

Senior Manager - Leveraging his knowledge

I've worked with many managers to codify their knowledge into vivid messages and supporting explanations, including authors, scientists, school principals, creative directors, sales managers and CEOs. Here's an example of how it works with the Head of Content at a radio network.

The Head of Content oversees multiple radio stations and literally

100s of breakfast teams, drive shows and the personalities who connect with millions of listeners every day. Whatever you think of commercial radio, the quantity of new ideas they create is staggering.

How many TV stations produce live content 24 hours a day? None. Putting a breakfast show together that will entertain, connect with audiences and help decode the world is not easy. There are playful and silly segments, controversial segments and analyses of politics, sport and local current affairs. These shows and the teams that run them do not come together by accident.

How to codify and leverage your knowledge

The Head of Content had accumulated many frequent flyer miles helping his team create quality on-air content. Each conversation was different, as each team is at a different stage of development. No matter how effective you are one-on-one, we all have a limited number of hours in each day. So, the question is; how to get his knowledge out to as many people as possible?

The first thing we did was **codify his knowledge** into short presentations. For example, 'How to create high-performing on-air teams in 3 steps'. As simple as that may sound, it was never conveyed as a 3-step process before. In a nutshell, these 3 steps are:

1. **Select the talent** (this is an <u>art</u> in identifying who will work well together).

2. **Build the ecosystem** (this is a <u>practical</u> approach to putting the right support team of producers, station managers and others to support the team).

3. **Promote the brand of the show** (with a list of <u>steps and strategies</u>).

Almost instantly, everyone in the organisation had access to his packaged knowledge. This gave him great leverage and increased the perceived value of his role.

The simplicity and flexibility of the 3-part structure, made it easy to convey different versions of his 'codified knowledge presentation'. The '30-second message' for spoken conversations went something like this;

'You create high-performing on-air teams by getting these 3 steps right; select the talent, build the ecosystem and promote the brand of the show.'

Imagine the speaker ticking off 1 finger at a time as he delivered this message over and over. Then, use all means available to convey the details within each step. A more detailed version can be shared with people in a document. A highly detailed version for training. Snippets can be cut into videos. And longer presentations for a speech or conference. All without changing the structure! Only the level of detail changes to suit the situation.

More impact with less effort

Everyone had access to his method to create a high-performing on-air team and new employees were brought up to speed more efficiently and effectively. Leveraging your knowledge in this way has powerful flow-on effects. You use less effort to get your ideas across, yet the ideas are easier to follow and more people have access to them.

These 'packaged knowledge' presentations have resulted in many of my clients being recognised as experts, and asked to make speeches at conferences around the world.

This increases the individual's personal brand as well as the brand of the organisation, which can help attract talented people.

MESSAGING PROMOTES YOUR ORGANISATION

Richard Branson - Nervous, but doesn't mind

Richard Branson is another master of the message. Even though he says 'uhm' and 'ah' when he speaks; and is often busy popping champagne or jumping from a hot air balloon, he always delivers short, catchy messages.

Whether it's Virgin Money, Virgin Atlantic or any business in the Virgin Group, journalists always get a clear message. He is a genius at getting the media to come *to him* so he can deliver messages about his business.

For example, Branson recently hosted a party to launch new flights between Australia and South Africa. And Sir Richard didn't disappoint. By taking his shirt off and dressing 'African', he got journalists attention. But his real goal is to get his messages published - preferably as the headline. Let's see how he did. Here are the headlines covering this event:

> *'Branson in Australia to promote new V Australia Johannesburg services.'*

> *'Branson's Safari party to Launch VA's Africa flights.'*

> *'Richard Branson says his Melbourne experience just like The Hangover movie.'*

Oh well, 2 out of 3 ain't bad. In the 3rd headline, the Herald Sun decided to lead with his comment about how drunk Branson was at last year's Grand Prix. But it was still a message success, under the headline they dutifully printed all the key messages he gave them.

Dropping messages in normal conversation

Branson had great success with a transferable message a few years ago. When he launched Virgin Home Loans, he received a huge amount of FREE publicity by appearing on TV shows. In between stories about space flights and balloon records, he casually sold his new business. Vivid Message number 1:

> *"Well, we're launching this business because you told us you felt the banks were ripping you off with fees."*

Followed by more chatter with the show's host. Then an engaging example:

> *"When I fly into Melbourne and Sydney I notice that all the big buildings are owned by the banks."*

Implying the banks are making too much money from you. Then Vivid Message number 2:

> *"A Virgin mortgage can save the average homeowner $30,000."*

Branson's conversational style shows that his preparation involves getting real clarity about his messages; not trying to script an entire conversation.

I heard people repeating these messages (virtually word for word) the following days. They found the ideas so compelling they did Branson's marketing for him, by passing on his messages during general conversation! This is Word-of-Mouth Marketing and is the most powerful of all forms of marketing. (Tip: This rarely happens if your message is too long.)

Being nervous or uncomfortable doesn't matter

So, Branson is a master at leveraging the media using messaging. Great. However there is an interesting aspect about his example.

Sir Richard Branson gets nervous in front of the camera and when speaking in public. He's spoken about his speaking anxiety publicly and written about it in his autobiography.

But it doesn't matter. It doesn't bother him that public speaking bothers him (if you get my meaning). This is a good way to reduce the impact of public speaking anxiety. You know it's there but you don't add a layer of frustration or drama over the top of it.

Yes, perhaps there are physical symptoms, like pounding heart, shaking or blushing. But instead of getting lost in those symptoms, you focus your attention on delivering your message or explaining your ideas, and the anxiety dissolves a little.

You might be surprised how many successful speakers still get nervous. However, it's not a big problem when you realise that it's not a big problem (more on controlling anxiety in Principle 5, later in the book).

The 'Hot Tub Ski Lodge' marketing message

One of the most enjoyable marketing messages I've worked on focused on a huge, old wooden hot tub, high on the snow covered mountains of Falls Creek.

I love to ski. And there's nothing more enjoyable than soothing aching muscles in a hot tub at the end of the day. Particularly if it's outside where you can see the stars and watch snow flakes melt on the rising steam.

Twenty years ago there weren't many hot tubs above the snow-line in Australia. That's why I loved staying at Pfeffercorn lodge. It had a magnificent outdoor spa made out of a massive wine barrel, cut in half.

I became friends with the owner and he would often talk about the challenges he had promoting his property. He had 2 marketing challenges as I saw it.

How to stand out from the crowd?

The first challenge was that nothing about his marketing stood out. It talked about the location on the mountain, size of the lodge, the fun of skiing, number of bedrooms, sleeping options available, etc. Fine. But so did everybody else. It was seen as just another accommodation option.

Built in 1965, Pfefforkorn was a classic, small ski lodge. It's position was nothing special, in the middle of the village, and it was older and smaller than many other chalets.

The second challenge was the name, 'Pfefforkorn'. It was hard to spell and pronounce. This is important. Word-of-mouth message transfer is a big part of any successful idea. The awkward-sounding name made it harder for friends to pass the marketing message on to others.

One day, as a few of the guests and I were warming our bones in the hot tub, the owner pulled out a brochure to get my opinion. The conversation went something like this:

Owner: What do you think of the new brochure?

Me: It's too cluttered and has no key message. Why not make the hot tub the focus? It's the thing that sets you apart.

Owner: Well, it is mentioned here on line 12...

Me: Yes, but why not make the whole focus about the hot tub. Rave about the world famous Pfefforkorn spa! Spend 70% of your brochure on this. Paint a picture of how people can warm their bones when it's cold outside. Show that it's the coolest hot tub on the planet, made from a huge old wine barrel...

Owner: But what about all the other important information?

Me: Put the details in small print. People know they can ski here. They know you're at Falls Creek. They know you've got beds. Give them 1 vivid message mate!

To cut a long story short, he did. And the marketing worked it's arse off. People started talking about 'that lodge at Falls Creek with the fabulous hot tub'. They would repeat the wine barrel story to their friends because it was interesting to talk about.

After a while, the hot tub became famous. In 2004 the old Pfefferkorn lodge was knocked down and replaced by a new development, Huski lodge. Guess what key selling point found it's way into the Huski sales brochure:

"We will retain the hot tub, which was once a feature out the front of Pfefferkorn, for Huski's day spa clientele."

Is your lodge the one with the hot tub?

Falls Creek now has more hot tubs per capita than most ski mountains. Older properties have added them, and newly built properties include them. Why? Because every chalet wanted to be able to answer the question that was regularly being asked of them, 'Is your lodge the one with the hot tub?'

CSIRO - Securing science funding

Your message is a doorway to the details of your subject.

The CSIRO (Commonwealth Scientific and Industrial Research Organisation) has 19 divisions. It's led and managed predominantly by scientists. However, they need to get funding from non-scientists - politicians.

This was a constant challenge as the scientists would often speak in so much detail that the politicians' eyes would glaze over and they would suddenly remember they had to be somewhere else.

One of the divisions asked me to run a messaging session. They had a problem. Their division generated 20% of the revenue for the CSIRO, but only received 5% of the funding.

What's the message for a non-scientist?

It was a communication problem. I spoke to the chief of this division and he said, "Even though we are arguably the most successful division, *no one really knows what we do*. It's not as simple as 'We created WIFI networking or we reduce manufacturing costs'. We have a complicated message."

So we gathered the senior people from this division into a room to clarify a super-simple message. A message that could be understood by a non-scientist.

Initially, there was resistance from the scientists about using nontechnical language. However, ultimately they realised they needed to speak in the language of their target audience (i.e. politicians), to secure funding. The message (that answered the question 'What does your division do?') became:

"We make cool new materials..."

Yes, the scientists agreed to use the word 'cool'! Remember, a message is a doorway to the details of your subject. Their simple message was then followed by a range of examples based on each person's area of expertise. So, they answer the question 'What does your division do' with, *"We make cool, new materials..."*

> *"...for example, smart plastics that can breathe - to make contact lenses that don't hurt your eyes."*

> *"...like super-thin and super-strong plastics used in artificial heart valves or plastic bank notes."*

> *"...such as new molecules for drugs that help the drugs work more effectively."*

By having this simple focus of 'cool new materials' as **a doorway to the details**, the scientists were able to have more interesting, relevant and *shorter* conversations with non-scientists, and help them understand what they did in just a few seconds.

The Pope Francis effect

Wow. What an impact Pope Francis has made on the image of the Catholic Church. Their messaging has been haphazard for many decades. The Catholic Church's basic message until 1962 was, 'we must follow the rules set down centuries ago' and the Church's role was seen as 'teachers of that law'.

A 50 year-old message

From 1962-65, the church conducted the 'Second Vatican Council' (Vatican II) to review relations between the Church and the modern world. It was revolutionary for it's time and moved the Catholic Church slightly away from this posture of 'the law'. Many rules and regulations were dismissed as unnecessary. Flexibility took the place of rigidity.

However, the messaging around this change was vague. In their great book *Positioning: The Battle for Your Mind*, Al Ries and Jack Trout

(1981) argued that 'What was painfully lacking was a clear representation of what the new Church was about.'

No-one had distilled what had transpired in Vatican II into simple messages. 'Opening the windows' was the strongest message to be associated with Vatican II as Pope John XXIII often said that it was 'time to open the windows of the Church to let in some fresh air'.

A little vague.

If you are not the teacher of the law, what are you?

The faithful asked, 'If you are not the teacher of the law, what are you?' For years, no simple answer was forthcoming. The response to, 'What is the role of the Catholic Church in the modern world?', was never the same twice. Without a consistent message, the Church allowed confusion to reign and lost influence.

Ries and Trout called this message vacuum a 'crisis of identity'. They suggested a communications program to reposition the church and reconcile the widening gap between liberal and conservative Catholics. Without this, **the key perceptions were driven by *critics* of the church**.

Pope Francis has finally taken on the job. With a vengeance! He's delivered more repeatable messages in 2 years than all the Popes since 1965. He's officially one of the most quotable Vicars of Christ ever (Gehrrig, 2013). His growing popularity is driven by his frequent, quotable messages.

'Did you hear what the Pope said yesterday...?' is now a common thread of discussion. For example, he told La Vivilta Cattolica that the Church does not need to speak constantly about abortion, contraception and homosexuality because other issues – notably the duty to help those who are poor and marginalised – have been neglected. He even threw in a couple of metaphors for impact. He said,

> *The church's pastoral ministry cannot be obsessed with the transmission of a disjointed multitude of doctrines to be imposed insistently ... We have to find a new balance; otherwise, even the moral edifice of the Church is likely to*

fall like a house of cards, losing the freshness and fragrance of the gospel."

Under Pope Francis, the new message seems to be, 'We are here to help, with compassion and inclusion, not to condemn with rules and dogma.' He famously asked;

"Who am I to judge?"

...with regard to the church's view of gay members, he stated that;

'Caring for the poor does not make you a communist.'

He explained his view that;

"Evolution is real and God is no wizard" and "the Big Bang theory doesn't contradict the Christian belief in creation."

Above were the headlines in publications around the world. His actual words on this issue were:

"God is not a divine being or a magician, but the Creator who brought everything to life," Francis said. "Evolution in nature is not inconsistent with the notion of creation, because evolution requires the creation of beings that evolve."

So, Francis may not be as good at crafting short, memorable messages as journalists who write the headlines, but his messages are getting passed on, and that's what influences people's perception.

Signs of a 'Francis effect' abound. A recent Pew survey reported by the Washington Post finds Francis has a 60% approval rating worldwide, with 78% approval in the US, and 84% in Europe. In a poll in March 2014, 1 in 4 Catholics said they'd increased their charitable giving to the poor this year. Of those, 77% said it was due in part to the Pope.

Backlash?

Not everybody is happy with the rapid change of direction. So the debate is on and those with the clearest message will have a great advantage. For example, U.S. Cardinal Raymond Burke said of the pope's leadership:

"Many have expressed their concerns to me. … There is a strong sense that the church is like a ship without a rudder."

This is a catchy message as well. Pope Francis addressed the concerns with,

"God is not afraid of new things."

It will be interesting to see where this debate goes. The best messaging will have the advantage.

Messaging: The holy grail of communication

The holy grail of communication is a **transferable message**. One that is easily recalled, then passed on from one person to another. It's a bit like going viral, but you don't need social media to harness the power of a transferable message. You just need to clarify it, and deliver it to your audience.

This opens a simple path that let's you speak to a group with little effort. You can avoid the long and arduous path of traditional public speaking.

Think about what you want to be complimented on. It might feel nice to hear that people love the sound of your voice or think your slides are cool, however, the best compliment is when someone repeats your message as though it was their idea! The idea wins, so you win.

BAD MESSAGING...

© 2002 Ted Goff

"Snowballs? I thought we were
discussing coconuts."

The cake that cost a Federal election

There is an amazing example of the difference between a confusing message and vivid message in Australian politics. A question was asked of the Leader of the Liberal party in 1991 (John Hewson) about a new GST tax being proposed.

His answer cost him his job.

Five years later in 1996, the same question was asked of the *new* Liberal Party leader (John Howard). He won the next election and went on to be the second longest serving Prime Minister in Australian history.

Both leaders were attempting to sell a new tax (GST) to the Australian public. One failed and the other succeeded. Here's exactly what was said.

Journalist: "If I buy a birthday cake with the GST, do I pay more or less for it?"

Leader of the Australian Liberal Party (1991):

"Well, it will depend whether cakes today in that shop are subject to sales tax or they're not, firstly, and they may have a sales tax on them. Let's assume that they don't have a sales tax on them and that birthday cake is going to be sales tax free, then of course, you wouldn't pay, it would be exempt, there would be no GST on it under our system. To give you an accurate answer, I need to know exactly what type of cake to give a detailed answer."

Result: The Liberal Party lost the election and the leader lost his job. Five years later that same journalist asked the new leader the same question. It was seen as the litmus test for whether a GST tax would be accepted.

Journalist: "If I buy a birthday cake with GST, do I pay more or less for it?"

New leader of the Liberal Party (1996):

"It will go up by between 2 and 4 per cent - but you'll have more money in your pocket to buy it due to (other) tax cuts."

Result: The Liberal Party won the election and all Australians now benefit from this wonderful tax.

Not only does the second version answer the question, it includes a new, persuasive idea; the extra cost of the tax will be more than covered by newly implemented tax cuts.

The first message used 90 words and failed to provide a useful answer. The second message used 27 words and not only answered the question clearly, it **defused the main concern about it.**

When it comes to communication, people want quality, not quantity. Don't deliver your information by the barrel, serve it by the glass.

IBM didn't 'Think'

IBM is famous for the word 'think'. You might recall their laptops were called 'ThinkPads' and desktop computers called 'ThinkStations'. IBM's founders posted the 'THINK' message in large letters on the walls to remind everybody to do that thing which Henry Ford described as 'the hardest work there is' (thinking).

It was a ubiquitous message that permeated the IBM culture. But it ultimately failed the company in a spectacular way.

What exactly do you want me to think?

The problem is that the single word 'THINK' is a vague message. It will mean different things depending on the perspective of the listener. Can you imagine an IBM manager saying to a member of his team, "Are you *thinking*, Joe?". What would your response be? "Oh yeah. Big time!"

Of course you are thinking, but there is no specific context.

What was lost over time was the fact that the focus of the IBM culture when it was wildly successful was a 2-word version of this message:

'Think ahead'.

This is a much clearer message. It focuses your attention and can be measured. And this message makes sense in the computer industry where changes in technology can make you obsolete very quickly. According to *Time* magazine: 'Fearful of falling behind in the fast-changing industry, CEO Tom Watson Jnr promoted 'scratchy, harsh' individuals and pressured them to *think ahead* …'

The worst business decision of all time?

The clear 2-word message, 'think ahead', and the culture it helped create, worked well for many years. IBM grew at an exponential rate in the 1950s and 60s.

However, by the 1970s, the 'ahead' part of the message was lost and IBM made perhaps the worst business decision of all time. A mistake that was the exact opposite of 'thinking ahead'.

Apple's 1977 launch of the first 'personal computer' caught IBM napping. They thought only hobbyists would buy it and ignored it for 3 years. Finally, watching the parabolic sales growth, they realised they needed to release an IBM Personal Computer (PC).

But the CEO didn't want to wait the 2 years needed to develop an IBM PC from scratch, so to save time and get their new PC to market quickly, they farmed out a couple of components.

They asked Intel to create the microprocessor and a *tiny* company called Microsoft to come up with the 'Operating System'. They accepted a deal from Bill Gates with 2 incredible provisions:

1. IBM wouldn't buy the operating system (DOS), but *license* it and Microsoft would retain ownership.

2. Microsoft would have the right to sell DOS to other computer manufacturers.

What happened? Firstly, the IBM PC was initially a massive success. By the mid 1980s the IBM PC was the dominant personal computer, beating Apple by a wide margin.

However, just a few years later IBM was basically broke. Microsoft was licensing DOS and Windows to anybody.

Computer *hardware* became a commodity business. Why pay double for an IBM PC, when a Dell PC had the same operating system and ran the same programs? IBM couldn't compete. They nearly went bust and ultimately sacked 200,000 people!

The epilogue to this story is that once dominant IBM sold their *loss-making* PC division to a Chinese company called Lenovo in 2005. There is no such thing as an IBM PC any more.

Too many messages are vague and open to multiple interpretations. In the IBM example, adding just 1 word made a significant difference.

Confusing Bushfire Warning - 'stay or go'

We've seen that 1 word can make a big difference in the 'Think' and 'Think Ahead' message. Here's another example. One that relates to the tragic bush-fires in Victoria in 2009, known as Black Saturday, when over 170 people died.

After the tragedy, many commentators, and a Royal Commission, discussed whether the headline message issued by the state fire authority ('stay or go') could have been clearer. 'Stay or go' doesn't guide your thinking clearly. It simply states that there are 2 options. It gives no guidance as to which option an individual should choose, or why.

Unfortunately the headline message was too short. The actual policy for community safety in bush-fires was entitled, 'Prepare, Stay and Defend or Leave Early', but it was deemed too long as a headline message and became known as 'Stay or go'. Our messages need to find the right balance between detail and brevity. For example, here are 3 options for the headline message:

'Stay or go'

'Stay, or go early'

'Stay and defend, or go early'

Which would you choose?

Let's face it, fire safety authorities have a significant challenge communicating to people who live in fire-prone areas. They need to jolt people into action, which requires a simple 'cut through' message. But, as the Royal Commission pointed out, they also need to remind people that their decisions when facing a fire depend on a lot of factors, and aren't as simple as a choice between staying or going.

"The Commission understands the attraction of an uncomplicated policy framework that presents two clear options – stay or go – but such an approach is simplistic. Realistic advice is unavoidably more complex and requires subtlety."

This is a serious subject but it highlights the choices we have to make when crafting a vivid message. Shorter is easier to remember, but provides less clarity. A longer version provides more clarity but may reduce recall. And adding or changing 1 word can make a significant difference.

Ultimately you need to use your own judgement to find the right balance.

Format Wars: Blu-Ray versus HD-DVD - can you put it in a sentence?!

Successful messaging flows easily in normal conversation.

Did you know that Blu-Ray was the winner of an Optical Disc Format War? The current Blu-Ray standard, promoted by Sony, beat out a rival format from Toshiba. The war raged for 3 years between 2006-2008, and was ultimately won by the Blu-Ray Disc.

There are a few theories about why the 'Blu-Ray' format beat out Toshiba's 'HD-DVD' format. Many people say that Blu-Ray won because it was included in Xbox and Playstation, which meant there were more Blu-Ray players in the hands of consumers, and as a result the movie studios and technology companies chose Blu-Ray.

I believe there is another far more fundamental factor at play: you can't use the term 'HD-DVD' in normal conversations without getting confused.

The reason is that both parts of the name already mean something else. 'HD' was already in widespread use as a term to represent **High Definition** in TVs, computer screens, cameras, digital video format, etc.

HD is also used as an abbreviation for the **Hard Drives** *within* computers, cameras, etc. The term 'HD' is overused and therefore open to misunderstanding and confusion.

And so is 'DVD'!

Try this now. Imagine you're at a store and you're having a conversation to learn more about the new format. Say this sentence out loud:

> *'Hi. I want to know if **HD-DVD** will work with my HD TV and DVD?'*

Say what?! Now try this sentence out loud:

> *'Hi. I want to know if **Blu-Ray** will work with my HD TV and DVD?'*

Much clearer. Technology can still be confusing, however Blu-Ray is a distinctly different word, so there is less chance for conversational stupefaction. Here's another conversation,

> *'Will **HD-DVD** be backward compatible with DVDs?'*

Or,

> *'Will **Blu-Ray** be backward compatible with DVDs?'*

These simple conversations only scratch the surface of the kinds of technical discussions that were also going on during the battle for format supremacy.

The conversations using the term Blu-Ray seemed more *concrete*. The individuals talking about this format sounded clearer and more certain when they used the Blu-Ray term compared to those who used the HD-DVD language. I can imagine HD-DVD people having to correct themselves more often because of the extra concentration required to make sense.

You can decide for yourself how important the name choice was. The point here is that when you test your messages, you want to make sure they *flow in normal conversation.*

What's next?

So hopefully you're now thinking; 'That's great, Cam. I see the value of being a message master. But is there a step-by-step method that will answer all my other questions and fill all the gaps required to be a great speaker?'

Yes! There is. It's called The Vivid Method for Public Speaking.

Let's look at that now.

THE VIVID METHOD FOR PUBLIC SPEAKING

Welcome to the practical part of this book! Glad you're still here. The following pages contain a method to prepare and deliver compelling speeches and presentations.

It's estimated that around 50,000 presentations are made around the world every *minute*. That's around 2 billion each month. Important decisions are made as a result. Projects are approved or cancelled. Tenders are granted. Hiring decisions and promotions are made.

Unfortunately, many of these presentations fail to engage their audience. Speakers struggle to translate their ideas in a way their audience can understand. As a result, bad decisions are made and the progress of careers is jeopardised. It all adds up to an enormous waste of time, money and talent.

The Vivid Method will guide you through both the planning and the delivery of great speeches and presentations. But first, we need to clear away some of the myths that might be complicating your public speaking...

PUBLIC SPEAKING MYTHS...

Body language: everything you know is wrong

Body language can be telling. However, most of us have been exposed to a dumb idea about the link between body language and public speaking impact. This dumb idea says that our non-verbal communication is more important than the words we say, no matter what the situation.

'More than 90% of impact is non-verbal' – not!

In the 2005 movie *Hitch,* Will Smith's character is a 'date doctor' who helps men find the love of their life. At one point he refers to a 'well-known statistic' to help his client seem more confident and intelligent - that 90% of one's impact comes from body language and vocal tone. Only 10% comes from the words we say.

This misunderstood statistic has become the damaging dogma within thousands of books and courses on communication. The specific figures that *appear* to backup this claim state that when speaking in public:

- 55% of the impact is conveyed via visual signs, e.g. facial expressions, body language and physical appearance.
- 38% of the impact is via your tone of voice.
- 7% of the impact is the words you say.

These numbers, particularly the last one – that our words have only a minor impact – have been quoted by public speaking 'experts' all over the world for 40 years. They have played a significant role in the overemphasis on 'performance' over natural style – ultimately making public speaking seem more complicated than it needs to.

But it's a myth.

WRONG.

A complete distraction.

The numbers themselves come from the work of Dr Albert Mehrabian, who published them in his 1971 book *Silent Messages*. Mehrabian was a respected professor who did credible research. However, the meaning attributed to the figures was taken out of context. It's just plain wrong when applied to public speaking in general.

I was taught these figures in that public speaking course I attended all those years ago, which caused me so much grief. But when I finally recognised that it made no sense, I contacted Dr Mehrabian directly. The first thing I discovered was that he was frustrated that his work has been so widely misunderstood. Very few people who use his figures have actually read his book or understand their context! Dr Mehrabian told me:

> "*These figures are only relevant when there is a contradiction - when your words are <u>contradicted</u> by your non-verbals.*"

Then he asked: "Do you have a credit card?"

Pause… "Um, yes, Visa", I responded.

"Would you like to buy a copy of the book?"

"Absolutely!"

So, he personally sent me a copy with a hand-written Post-It note at the start of Chapter 5.

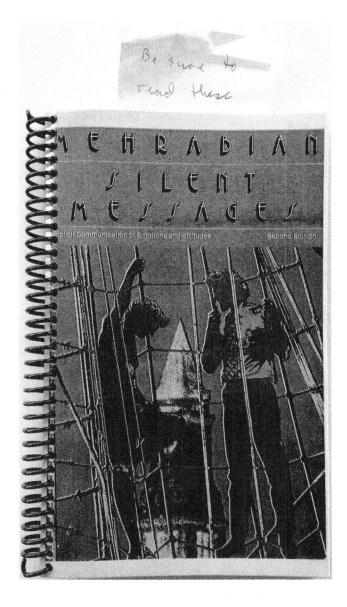

The note read, '*Please read these 5 pages*'. The chapter that dealt with the famous statistic was called '*The Double Edged Message*'. As soon as I read the chapter title, it all fell into place.

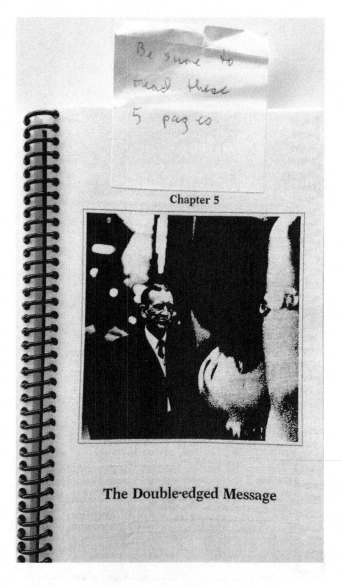

Be sure to read these 5 pages.

Chapter 5

The Double-edged Message

The chapter is about the *contradictory* messages we sometimes send out. For instance, imagine you are in the middle of an emotional conversation with your spouse. He or she has an eyebrow raised, hands planted firmly on hips, and through gritted teeth, says:

"No! I am NOT angry!"

Would you believe these words in this context?? Normally I'd demonstrate this story to an audience by putting my hand on my hip and actually screaming through gritted teeth. That way it's instantly obvious the words wouldn't be believed because they are said *with anger*. But you can see from the explanation that there is a contradiction between the words and the tone used.

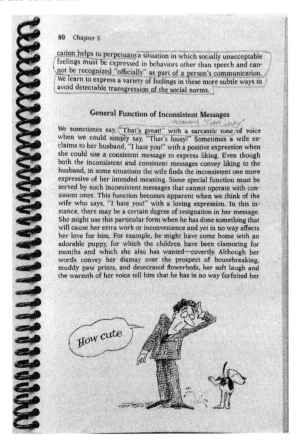

Put simply, if your visual signals and/or vocal tone contradict the words you are saying, the visual signals will be given more weight by your listener. Fine.

By the way, none of Mehrabian's research was based on speeches, presentations or any kind of public speaking! In fact, Mehrabian himself is so frustrated by the misunderstanding of his work, his personal website clearly states:

> *"Please note that this and other equations regarding relative importance of verbal and nonverbal messages were derived from experiments dealing with communications of feelings and attitudes (i.e., like–dislike). Unless a communicator is talking about their feelings or attitudes, these equations are not applicable."*

The real message is 'Be yourself'

In my opinion, the real message from Dr Mehrabian's research seems to be: *'be yourself'*. Trying to be something you're not might lead to giving off these contradictory messages.

This is insanely ironic, don't you think? A man does painstaking research, which shows us that contradictory messages will weaken your impact and confuse your audience. Thousands of experts misread that data and teach people that they need to change their style, change who they are, sometimes in a dramatic fashion, to be effective in front of an audience. This puts people into such turmoil that they give off contradictory messages!!

How important is body language in public speaking?

Your body language matters because it either supports what you're saying or contradicts it.

You may be thinking, what about TV shows like 'The Mentalist' or 'Lie to Me' where the hero is able to divine what people are thinking through body language signals? Isn't there some magic influence around body language components that I need to learn?

Well, it depends. (Probably not.) Consider the following examples.

Mr Body Language – Alan Pease

I love Alan Pease. He has been known as 'Mr Body Language' since he published his first book on the subject in 1981. He's clever, funny and an entertaining speaker. I've chatted to him a few times at the National Speaker's Association.

He and his wife Barbara also wrote and published the 10 million copy best seller, *Why Men Don't Listen and Women Can't Read Maps* which pulls together research on the differences between men and women. It's funny and interesting because there is some underlying truth to it.

In his body language books, he also pulls together research that has an underlying truth in certain circumstances. He explains techniques such as not touching your nose (it means you are lying), keeping your palms up (you will be seen as non-threatening and people will respond positively to you), keeping your fingers together (you will be seen as authoritative), keeping your elbows out (you will be perceived as powerful and strong), keeping your distance (so people won't lean away from you because they're irritated) and mirroring others' body language (you will build rapport quickly).

These insights have some truth to them in certain situations. And Alan Pease presents them in an interesting and amusing way. But they certainly can't be relied on to be true in all situations.

And if you tried to follow them all, you risk looking awkward or devious, as these techniques take you out of the moment and into mechanical, thought-driven and unnatural movements.

Consider Alan's *Body Language Book*. The table of contents alone goes for 9 pages and has 270 headings! They include:
- The head nod
- The head shake
- The head shrug
- The basic head positions
- Why you should learn to nod
- Wearing glasses on the head
- Peering over the glasses
- The four main standing positions
- The cowboy stance
- Straddling a chair
- How we move from closed to open
- The European leg cross

- The American figure four
- And 260 more…

Imagine the confusion and uncertainty trying to decide which ones to apply! Don't you think they might interrupt your natural train of thought?

The original science of body language

There have been a number of respected researchers who have looked into the impact of nonverbal communication over the years. Anthropologist Ray Birdwhistell, founded Kinesics as a field of inquiry in 1952. He studied the meaning of animal and human facial expression, gestures, posture and gait, and visible arm and body movements.

Even though he famously stated that 'no more than 35% of the social meaning of a conversation or an interaction is carried by the words', he also knew that body language could not be interpreted or orchestrated to have *a fixed meaning*. Here is how *The Dictionary of Anthropology* (1997) summarises his position:

> *"Birdwhistell pointed out that 'human gestures differ from those of other animals in that they are polysemic, that they can be interpreted to have many different meanings depending on the communicative context in which they are produced".*

And,

> *"He resisted the idea that 'body language' could be deciphered in some absolute fashion."*

And that,

> *"Every body movement must be interpreted broadly and in conjunction with every other element in communication."*

This is sooo important. Whenever an expert speaking coach tells you something like: 'Research shows that 'X' gesture, movement or action will have 'Y' impact', they are not being accurate.

What they should be saying is 'Research indicates it's possible in some circumstances that 'X' gesture, movement or action will have 'Y' impact, but the only thing we know for certain is that this **won't be true** for everybody or in every situation'.

How to get on TV as a body language expert

Unfortunately for these experts, this correct explanation won't get them on TV as a body language expert. But there are plenty of 'experts' on TV who are willing to state incorrectly that 'X' body language absolutely means 'Y' result.

Given that everybody is different and every speaking situation is unique, context is key. The point is, body language theories won't make you a great speaker.

Your rough edges might be OK!

We teach public speaking to thousands of people every year and we have never had a phone call from a client asking us to make all their speakers *the same*.

The opposite is true.

Clients call and say: "We just sat through a 2-day conference and every speaker had the same orchestrated style and it drove us to tears. Please help…"

Maybe your imperfect speaking style is just what the audience needs to be engaged. Consider the following example.

Bill Gates persuades Congress with bad body language

While I was researching the truth about public speaking some years ago, I saw a fascinating example of the focus on body language playing out in the United States Congress.

Today, companies like Apple, Samsung and Google are so powerful in the computer space, few people remember how dominant Microsoft was in 1997. They had so much power and market share the US Congress labeled them a monopoly and decreed Microsoft be split into two companies (one for the Windows operating system and another for applications).

Bill Gates, CEO of Microsoft at the time, was hit with many questions as he sat on a lonely chair being grilled by members of

Congress. In response, he made short presentations arguing his position. Daily progress of these Congressional hearings was reported by TV, Financial news networks and technology shows.

I followed this closely. It was puzzling to see that many headlines and commentary focused on Gates' body language. They talked about how he sat, how long he took to respond to questions and how he rocked in his chair awkwardly. If you read the headlines and listened to this commentary, you'd believe that Gates was getting hammered in the sessions and Congress was winning the argument. But this was just a silly side-show.

Gates won the argument

While all this attention was placed on his body language, people lost focus on the real story – his explanations, his arguments, his message. Bill Gates was excellent in this regard. And he won the argument! His supposedly 'awkward' body language did not weaken those messages.

Did Microsoft get split in two? No. Gates' style may not have been perfect from the 'performance' viewpoint, but it didn't need to be. Although the (misdirected) body language commentary seemed to think otherwise.

So, am I saying body language doesn't matter? No. It matters a lot. It supports and reinforces what you say. I'm suggesting there is a better way to achieve natural, compelling body language - let it flow instinctively from the clarity of your message and the ease of your natural style.

Why do we keep making the same robotic mistakes?

There was an important attempt to understand the impact of non-verbal communication in France in the 1800s. Francois Delsarte was born in 1811 and studied arts at the Paris Conservatory, but was disappointed with the *posed style* of acting they taught. So he started observing people, particularly in public places, to see how they actually moved and responded to *real life* situations.

He wanted acting and stage performance to more naturally reflect real life – as opposed to the wooden acting that existed at the time. He observed certain *patterns of expression* associated with voice, breath and movement. He was interested in the physical gestures that indicated emotions, yet recognised the difficulty in replicating them when acting because they're not the actor's real emotions.

He developed what he called 'the Science of Applied Aesthetics'. Essentially an acting style that attempted to *connect* the inner emotional experience of the actor with a set of gestures and movements to accurately convey those emotions to the audience.

More irony - his aim was freedom of movement

Delsarte was attempting to teach people how to **release restrictions** and free their movement to *convey feelings accurately* - and thus connect with an audience. Cool. Unfortunately, Delsarte didn't write a book explaining his method. However, 14 years after his death in 1871, *The Delsarte System of Expression* was published by the *student* of one of Delsarte's *students*, and it became a wild success.

The problem was that the key idea from Delsarte's actual work - that the gestures should flow from within, from the connection to the actual emotions - was lost. And the *opposite idea* drove the training.

By the 1890s, The Delsarte System was being taught all over the world, particularly in America, by teachers who didn't understand the emotional connection underpinning the movements. Soon, the **teaching of gestures** and body language became just mechanised poses. The exact problem Delsarte set out to change!

Stephen Wangh concluded, in his book on *A Physical Approach to Acting*, 'It led others into stereotyped and melodramatic gesticulation, devoid of the very heart that Delsarte had sought to restore.'

When you make a speech or presentation, it's your belief, your certainty about your idea that engages your audience. Not amateur acting skills. Getting comfortable in your own skin and getting clear in your mind about what you are saying are the keys. Not to clutter your mind with techniques, cut and pasted onto your talk.

The point: Don't worry about orchestrating body language.

The other 7 Public Speaking Myths

There are a number of other obstacles that can waste your energy and reduce your impact when speaking, because they add confusion, uncertainty and even guilt. Let's dissolve them now. I've listed them here as seven myths.

Myth 1: Bad first impressions can't be overcome

Have you heard that audiences form their lasting impression in the first 30 seconds? Or the first 8 seconds?

This is very misleading. It implies that the lasting impression of your talk won't be your wisdom, the clarity of your message or the relevance of your information; it all rests on the first few seconds. People believe that if they make a mistake at the start they won't be able to recover.

What pressure! Public speaking is not that hard. Or mysterious.

There are many versions of the first impression myth. Most recently, Malcolm Gladwell's popular book, *Blink: The Power of Thinking Without Thinking*, promoted the idea that spontaneous or unconscious impressions are as good as carefully considered ones.

However, the book was criticised by a range of researchers, including Nobel prize winner Daniel Kahneman, author of *Thinking, Fast and Slow*. He stated that Gladwell's book created the impression that intuition is magical, which he argues is false.

So what's the reality? No matter how you slice it, the first few seconds will only ever form a *first* impression, not a *lasting* impression.

Look at how this myth stacks the cards against you. Imagine you're about to stand up in front of an audience and you believe that first impressions are everything. We know that nerves are typically strongest at the start, because that's the point of most uncertainty. So what happens if you stumble on a word or trip on a cord or forget part of your intro at the start?

In your mind it's a disaster because the first 30 seconds have gone poorly and you're thinking 'I can't recover!' So you tighten up, feel more nervous, think less clearly and forget the next point. You believe all is lost and act accordingly - and end up making *a series of* bad impressions.

Just remember, the audience's impression of you is developed and reinforced throughout your entire talk. I've known many speakers who've started awkwardly, and wowed them by the end. You don't need to sabotage yourself just because you have a challenge at the start. Let yourself off the hook. Laugh it off.

In fact, making 'a save' can form a greater connection with the audience *after* a problem. When a joke bombs, a good comedian acknowledges it and laughs it off. In the same way, you can 'make a save' by smiling, and naming the problem in front of the audience so *they* get that *you* get what the problem is. (Got that?!) This point of recognition releases the tension and the problem dissolves.

For example, the technology doesn't work. You smile and say something like 'This is not working'. You talk about something else while the problem is fixed and then you continue.

When you smile at the problem, name it, and the audience smiles at the problem too, you're viewing the problem *together*. That's a connection with your audience. Many presenters are polished and rehearsed but make no connection with their audience at all.

In other words, making a 'save' after a setback on stage, can actually give you more impact than a perfect, 'flawless' presentation. Don't focus on the mistakes, focus on the next line. Engage them with subsequent impressions and they will be left with a positive overall impression - no matter what happened in the first 30 seconds.

Myth 2: You must eliminate nerves to be a great speaker

Many people have a niggling thought; *'If I was a good speaker, I wouldn't get nervous. But I do get nervous, so I'm not good enough'.*

Some worry it's a sign of weakness to admit they get nervous, and this idea embeds itself into their mind creating more uncertainty every time they speak in public.

The reality is, it's normal to feel speaking anxiety, no matter how experienced or polished you are.

Richard Branson admits he gets nervous in public speaking situations and has done since he was a teenager. The nerves haven't held him back, he's one of the most sought-after speakers on the planet. I've worked with professional sportspeople and TV presenters, and they also get nervous before an important event. Football players, tennis players, as well as actors and musicians often have a pre-event ritual to manage their anxiety.

Nerves are normal, we just need to put them into perspective. Far from holding you back, anxiety can focus the mind and lead to a better result. Nerves don't need to be eliminated – they just need to be understood.

Myth 3: Good speakers don't use notes

Here's something I've heard from speakers who worry they're not good enough; *"Oh! He's such a good speaker - He didn't look at his notes once!"*

Who cares if you look at your notes?

Many people believe you can't be an accomplished speaker unless you're able to deliver a presentation without notes. In practice there is nothing wrong with using notes *if* they help you speak with clarity and certainty. The Steve Jobs 'Stanford Graduation Speech' was read from notes, yet it's one of the most famous speeches in the world, more popular than *any* TED talk.

Notes *can* be used poorly, of course. Particularly if you read a speech in a way that implies you're not familiar with the content. For example:

> *"Good morning. My name is Cam...*
>
> [pause to turn the page to read the next word]
>
> *Barber. And I'm excited to speak to you today about...*
>
> [pause to turn the page to read the next word]
>
> *clear communication."*

This is an exaggerated example of course, but some speakers using notes/slides make it seem like they're 'phoning it in.' The same applies to the use of TelePrompTers or auto-cues; they can be used well, but when used poorly the speaker appears lifeless and robotic. Checking your slides and then talking to the audience is fine, but planting your feet with your back to the audience and reading every word on your slides is not!

So, notes aren't a problem, it's how we use them.

Don't feel guilty about using notes. Everybody needs to find the right *balance* of notes to suit the event and the subject. Some professional speakers make one speech over and over. It's easier to jettison notes in this situation. Most business presenters are not in that position, so there's no point comparing yourself.

If notes give you greater clarity or certainty, use them. The way to find the right balance of notes and free talking is addressed in the Structure section of the Vivid Method.

Myth 4: Eliminate errors and you'll be a great speaker

Another unproductive idea is; 'if you eliminate every mistake you'll be a great speaker'. Training courses that follow this myth give you a list of mistakes to avoid. They might even record a video of you making these 'mistakes', show it to the rest of the class and get you to focus all your effort on eradicating them. The list often includes:

- Never say 'um'!
- Don't put your hands in your pockets.
- Use 'open' gestures, never 'closed' gestures.
- Don't move around the room too much (or too little!).
- Maintain eye contact for the optimum time.
- Pause for the optimum 3 seconds.
- Etc.

This myth wastes energy by overemphasising minor distractions and can create the kind of self-consciousness that leads to situations like the famous Michael Bay meltdown.

Do you know about the Michael Bay meltdown? Search it. While being interviewed on stage at the Consumer Electronics Show in Vegas in 2014, the successful Hollywood director missed a line and got out of synch with his auto-cue for about 3 seconds. He became so flustered and embarrassed that he walked off the stage in the middle of the interview - head bowed and tail between his legs. The audience and the interviewer were stunned.

Irony strikes again. The belief that small mistakes are a deal-breaker, can create an environment where you make *more* mistakes. Michael Bay believed he had to be mistake-free; this increased his anxiety to the point where he *created* an embarrassing result that was front page news all around the world. However, if he believed that stumbling on his words for a couple of seconds was irrelevant (which it is), he could have taken a moment and continued without incident.

Does it even follow that you'll be able to engage your audience more effectively by removing all rough edges from your speech? No. The *promise* you make to your audience in a business presentation is different to the promise you make if you put on a Broadway play. A Broadway play makes the promise that professional actors will learn a script perfectly and never make a mistake. This is just not the world of business presentations. Your promise to your audience is that the information will be relevant, useful, clear and show them the value of your idea. So what if you stumble on your words a couple of times.

Sure, it makes sense to reduce distractions like excessive use of 'ums' and 'ahs' - because they could reduce the impact of your explanations. (Although, if your talk is dull or hard to follow, the audience, in their boredom, might start to focus on distractions – like how often you touch your nose or say 'um'. However, if your ideas are compelling they won't notice or care about your fidgeting).

The impact of your 'rough edges' fits on a *sliding scale*. For example, if there are more 'ums' than words, your talk will be harder to follow. In the end you need to work out the right balance for your style. Real people often have idiosyncratic (even distracting) mannerisms, but these will be forgiven if you engage your audience.

So, damn the torpedoes! Full speed ahead with clarity of message and natural style, rough edges and all. Being clear and genuine is far more compelling than being perfect.

Myth 5: You need a particular kind of voice

Some people worry they can never be a successful speaker because their voice isn't 'right' for it. It's not true. Nor is the converse; having a beautiful 'radio voice' doesn't make you a good speaker.

When I coached a senior public servant with political aspirations she told me that five years previously, she was advised by a speaking expert that as a woman she needed to have a low timbre in her voice to demonstrate gravitas. And what did she get from this advice? Five years of second guessing every word she uttered and increasing public speaking anxiety as a result.

Even if this myth were true what should you do? Never speak again? And what are the consequences of trying to change your voice? Huge amounts of wasted effort and increasing paranoia.

Any voice can be compelling and credible if it is used with certainty.

Many radio announcers, with classic rich voices, have become business managers, but their voices don't give them any advantage over their 'off air' counterparts when it comes to seeking funding for their strategies or Board support for their projects. What wins support is a relevant message, not a pretty voice.

We've been exposed to historical speeches where the likes of Churchill and John F. Kennedy use stirring, theatrical voices. Martin Luther King Jr used dramatic tremors in his voice to build excitement in his *'I have a dream'* speech. But isn't the context a little different for your next business presentation? Do you think you'll have more impact with dramatic tremors in your voice trumpeting *"I.. have.. a.. spreadsheet..!"*

A *Barry White voice* might sound wonderful on a fur rug in front of a fire, but it won't give you an advantage at the yearly conference.

Myth 6: You need acting skills

We've talked about this. Yet so many presentation skills trainers are actors.

I recently coached the CEO of a company that hosts some of the world's best speakers. She was due to open for Jim Collins in front of 2,500 people and was nervous. She had put off dealing with her public speaking anxiety for years, but this was an important event and she wanted to shine.

Before we spoke, she had attended a 2-day course at NIDA, the National Institute of Dramatic Arts. The course was run by actors, as so many presentation skills courses are. She learnt some great breathing techniques, however the acting model added so much drama (pardon the pun) to public speaking, she was overwhelmed and uncertain by day 2.

Later, we had a coaching session that debunked the myths, removed the burden of competing with Brad Pitt and Angelina Jolie, and refocused her attention on what mattered - structuring her ideas, testing them out loud, and talking naturally. A few days later she opened the Jim Collins event with charm and humour!

Of course, that's just one person's experience. You might learn some useful stuff in an acting course: breathing, pausing, timing, stage presence and more. But ask yourself: what's the impression you're left with when actors run presentation courses? Does the comparison with professional actors send a message that public speaking is effortless? That you can be yourself when speaking? That you don't need to change who you are?

Or, is the implication that you need to be as good as someone who puts on a play at the Opera House? The acting skills requirement leaves many participants with rounded shoulders from the pressure, believing there is so much to learn to be good.

My suggestion is to focus on the easy way first (The Vivid Method in the 2nd half of this book) and then decide if you need to spend the time to add acting skills as cream on the cake.

The acting myth feeds a belief that delivering a presentation is more about performance than substance. Ironically, we've found that *reducing* the focus on performance improves delivery skills more quickly and with less effort.

Why?

Because you're not spending so much energy worried about 'performing', you get out of your own way and just explain your ideas. And amateur acting can look wooden or robotic, hindering your ability to connect with an audience.

The challenge of creating better business presentations won't be solved by better acting. It'll be solved with compelling messages and great explanations.

Myth 7: You must rehearse for hours

Practice! Practice! Practice! This is often touted as the secret to successful public speaking.

Of course practice is helpful. Testing your ideas out loud and refining your presentation increases clarity and builds certainty. However, we've found (from working with over 15,000 people) that a short rehearsal is usually better than a long rehearsal. You can build certainty with very little rehearsal time. (I'll show you the *1-minute rehearsal* later in the book.)

Over-rehearsing can be a problem, an obstacle to being *in the moment*. On the day, the voice inside our head compares what we are saying to our best rehearsal, rather than focusing on explaining our points *now*. Our attention is directed away, trying to remember the words we practiced, rather than being *present* and flowing in our explanations.

Also, there is a huge difference between *directed practice* and misdirected practice. For example, practicing with the intent to remember every word can waste a lot of time and energy. And this kind of practice can be tinged with the anxiety that accompanies the need for perfection. It's exhausting! Whereas directed practice can be almost effortless.

Most of my clients have decided that the best way to rehearse is NOT to remember it word-for-word. They practice the start, the end and key points. They get completely clear on the structure, the messages and where the explanations fit in the structure. Then they trust that they will be able to form engaging sentences on the day. Some clients like to do a run-through of the whole presentation or speech, particularly on a new subject, but never attempt to remember every word.

For many, the 1-minute rehearsal works best. Here are some of it's benefits over a full rehearsal:

It takes less time.

You can do it a few times with minimal effort.

Your presentation is mentally lighter and easier to remember.

The focus on key points and structure gives you more flexibility.

It reduces mental steps, so you avoid overwhelm.[1]

The 3 parts of the Vivid Method...

In today's world, there are few roles that allow you to completely avoid public speaking or presentations. If you shy away from public speaking, you miss opportunities to demonstrate your competence, your wisdom, your value.

Given that fear of public speaking is regularly ranked as people's number 1 fear, mastering it can expand your self-image and extend your range.

The Vivid Method simplifies public speaking and shows you how to dissolve the associated anxiety. You might also find that the tools to control anxiety can be applied in other areas of life.

The method has been designed to guide you step-by-step. It has 3 parts:

1. The **5 Principles** to control nerves and think clearly.

2. The **Speech Outline** process to clarify and structure your ideas.

3. Options to give **Great Explanations** and engage your audience.

---

[1] 'Overwhelm' is now a noun! I'll use the word 'Overwhelm' as a noun. I'm told it's a verb but if Shakespeare can invent new words, surely I can repurpose one that addresses the biggest issue many of us face this information overload age.

VIVID METHOD PART ONE: THE CLARITYFIRST PRINCIPLES

Ok, we've cleared away the myths. Now let's look at the principles that will help you think clearly and control nerves:

Principle 1: All anxiety is caused by uncertainty.

Principle 2: Message transfer is your measure of success.

Principle 3: We all have the closeness problem.

Principle 4: Your natural style is the right style.

Principle 5: You can control anxiety by understanding it.

PRINCIPLE 1: ALL ANXIETY IS CAUSED BY UNCERTAINTY

When I get phone calls from people who want coaching help for their big presentation, it often becomes clear that they are unsure what they will cover, unsure about what's expected of them at the event and/or unsure about their ability to do it well. In other words, they are full of uncertainty. The conversation might go something like this:

Cam:	"So, what's your speaking event?"
Caller:	"I just know it's a big industry thing and I need to impress. My PA has a brochure with the details."
Cam:	"What will you be speaking about?"
Caller:	"I haven't decided yet. There are many things I could cover."
Cam:	"What are others at the event speaking about?"
Caller:	"Good question. They might be listed in that brochure..."

You can see that there are multiple elements of *uncertainty* in the mind of the speaker – and each one generates anxiety. While some level of anxiety is normal and healthy, out-of-control anxiety is not normal or healthy and will reduce the impact of your presentation. And make it much less fun!

The first ClarityFirst principle is that *'All anxiety is the result of feelings of uncertainty'*. In other words, the more uncertainty you have about an upcoming presentation, the more nervous you're likely to feel.

The opposite is also true: the more you feel prepared, and the clearer you are about your subject, the venue and what your audience expects, the less nervous you will be.

Do you get nervous about being nervous?

It is hard to overstate the impact of uncertainty.

Research demonstrates that uncertainty can impact our physical strength, confidence in our proven abilities and even weaken our immune system.

One example of this is the work of psychologist Stanley Schachter. He set up an experiment in which participants were given a drug similar to adrenaline. The participants were then divided into two groups: one group was told to expect good feelings and given regular feedback that they were having the time of their lives during the experiment; the other group was told that the drug might bring on some bad feelings, and given feedback that the experience might be negative.

Despite the input (the drug) being identical for each group, those who expected good feelings and were given feedback that *made them feel certain about what was happening*, reported enjoying the rush of adrenaline. While the group that was filled with uncertainty and told they might have a bad experience reported feelings of negative anxiety.

Uncertainty weakens your mind and body

Another example is a simple muscle test. Imagine your name is Joe Smith. You hold one arm horizontally in front of you and say out loud, 'I am Joe Smith'. If I were to push down on your arm, your resistance (strength) would be high. If, on the other hand, you did the same thing but you said, 'My name is Angelina Jolie and I am an astronaut', I would feel much lower resistance when I pushed down on your arm. While uncertainty seems like a mental issue, it has a significant physical impact.

The challenge when preparing for a speech is that our mind can start posing questions that can't be easily answered. For example;

- How will I be judged?
- What if I forget something?
- What if I embarrass myself?
- Have I prepared well enough?
- What if I can't answer the questions?

If you don't resolve the uncertainty these questions generate they will magnify anxiety and the resulting physical symptoms: a pounding heart, shaking hands, feeling sick, a shaking voice, a dry mouth – the list goes on. Your mind and body can be overwhelmed.

Conversely, resolving questions like these ahead of time can *boost your energy and give you an enormous sense of direction* as you head into your presentation.

Of course, we can't have *complete* certainty about everything – and nor would we want it. 100% certainty in life would be pretty boring! We also need to be able to adapt to our audience's needs – their questions will vary from meeting to meeting, for instance. And we need to be able to adapt to something going wrong, such as the technology not working (more on that later).

Four ways to get more certainty

This principle is powerful because it's simple, it's universally true in life, and it kick-starts your brain to think about your speech *more consciously*. Say Principle 1 out loud now; "All anxiety is caused by uncertainty". A practical thought might pop into your head now; 'Mmm, what are the areas of uncertainty for *me*, for *this* particular presentation… and what can I do to get more certainty about them.'

Here are 4 areas to start with to increase the level of certainty going into a speech or presentation:

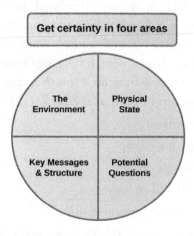

1. Know your speaking environment

What will the room be like? Will there be a stage? A lectern? What data projection equipment will be available? How will the chairs (and tables) be laid out? Will someone introduce you? Who speaks before and after you?

If you know the venue, great. If not, these questions can be answered by a visit to the venue before your talk or, a phone call to someone who can paint a clear picture for you. And don't be afraid to *send your preferences* to the organisers ahead of time; rather than just accepting the environment you are given; you can have some control over it.

A good example is microphones; some people are happy to stand behind a lectern and use the fixed microphones provided, while others (including me) are most comfortable with a wireless lapel or head microphone and the freedom to move around this provides.

What about the remote 'clicker' used to advance slides? Have you ever arrived at a venue and been handed something that looks like a television remote control, with 20 or 30 buttons? I've seen presenters take on a dazed expression as they try to work out the correct button to accomplish the simple task of moving to the next slide.

This adds uncertainty when there is a simple solution. Bring your own clicker. They are widely available, inexpensive and you'll always have certainty about how it works.

So, get more certainty about your speaking environment by asking questions. Get to the venue early to check out the room to test your technology and get a feel for the layout.

2. Get clear on key message and structure

We'll cover 'getting clear on message and structure' in Part 2 of the Method, so there's no need to go into it now. Suffice to say, plenty of delicious certainty is created when we're clear on message and structure.

3. Anticipate potential questions

This is an area that often throws highly prepared speakers. They put so much work into their *positive* argument, they don't consider the opposing view - and are not prepared to counter it when it comes up.

Their presentation goes beautifully … until they are put off balance by a difficult question. There's nothing worse than a speaker visibly surprised at a question, it appears they haven't thought their argument through.

Of course, some questions will be difficult to answer, but we never want to look shell-shocked or be at a loss for words. And we never have to be, because it only takes a few minutes to prepare for difficult questions.

The best way is to imagine a hostile person at the back of the room shouting out the hardest possible questions you can think of. Write the questions down. Write them in the most aggressive language you can imagine. There are generally no more than 2 to 5 big questions.

Now, next to the difficult questions, write your response. Some will be easily addressed and others harder to satisfy. It doesn't matter. At least you'll have a response, so you'll have greater certainty throughout a presentation and seem more confident and prepared. (I'll show you how to turn difficult questions into a positive later in the book under the heading 'You may be thinking …')

Don't hide from the possible difficult questions in the hope that they won't come – that's one way to ensure that they do get asked!

4. Understand your physical state

Your physical state means an awareness and understanding of the physical symptoms of anxiety you feel. Understanding how your body reacts to stress and anxiety is another way of getting more certainty. Rather than expecting to eliminate nerves completely, learn to recognise the symptoms of your nervousness, observe them *objectively* and come to terms with them. You can control your nerves by understanding them. We'll explore this fully in Principle 5.

Key point about uncertainty

The anxiety you feel before and during a presentation is a direct reflection of the amount of uncertainty you carry. The secret is to deal with the *causes* of anxiety, rather than trying to put band aids on the symptoms.

PRINCIPLE 2: MESSAGE TRANSFER IS YOUR MEASURE OF SUCCESS

Have you seen the movie *Pulp Fiction*? If you have, you might recognise the character named Butch, a boxer (played by Bruce Willis) who has double-crossed a crime boss, who is now trying to kill him.

He meets up with his girlfriend, who, following Butch's instructions, has packed their belongings to leave the country and make their escape. While looking through the possessions his girlfriend grabbed from their apartment, Butch notices his watch is not there.

Earlier in the movie it was convincingly demonstrated (in a hilarious scene with Christopher Walken) that this watch, handed down from his grandfather, to his father, to him, was the most valuable thing he owned. Money could replace everything else, but nothing could replace the watch - and his girlfriend had forgotten it.

Your listeners can't read minds

Butch is furious. He's a boxer and appears aggressive. He throws the television across the room, screams at his girlfriend, and then, just when you expect him to get more violent, he stops, swallows his anger and says:

> *"No, it's not your fault ... it's my fault. I didn't communicate to you that the watch is the one thing that was really important. How would you know that? You're not a mind reader."*

Butch had asked for 10 things to be done, and 9 of them were done perfectly. So his girlfriend could argue she got it 90% right. But this measure fails to reflect the communicator's intention.

As he drives back into mortal danger to get his watch, Butch punches the steering wheel and shouts to himself in frustration; *"There was only ONE THING I needed you to remember – the other stuff was unimportant"*. (Butch did finally get his watch back, but only after risking his life and leaving a trail of destruction.)

Whether we like it or not, the person delivering the message has the responsibility for what the listener *receives*. What should Butch's message have been? Perhaps something like,

> *"Whatever you do, don't forget the watch!"*

Maybe it should have been repeated to ensure its importance was conveyed. But the message was lost in all the other instructions he gave his girlfriend.

You might point out that his girlfriend should have paid more attention. Maybe. But that won't change the result. As leaders, managers and team members, if we don't make ourselves accountable for successful message transfer, *we* lose. Blaming the audience when they miss the point doesn't get us the result we need. Just an excuse to justify our communication failure.

Most presenters don't know their message

If there is one thing to be absolutely certain about every time you give a presentation, it's that *message transfer is your measure of success*. Nothing else matters if you fail to get your message across.

Not your gestures;

Not your slides;

Not the speed of your delivery;

Not your tone of voice or use of pauses;

Not how you stand or how much eye contact you have;

Not the way you look.

While all of these have some impact on the effectiveness of your presentation, you can get away with being imperfect *if you have a clear and relevant message*.

If this seems obvious (especially since I hammered this idea in the first half of this book), think about the presentations you have seen. Did the message stand out so clearly from the details that you wanted to repeat it to others?

© 2002 Ted Goff

"I don't have anything to say. Allow me to explain in detail."

In my experience I would say that most speakers don't know their message. Over the years I have asked thousands of people, just before they are about to speak: *"In one or two sentences, what is the message you want to leave with your audience? Give me the exact words."* Most are unsure, or respond without real clarity. The message is usually in the presentation *somewhere*, just lost in the detail.

This is a great pity, because they are smart people - intelligent, talented, and have great ideas to share. They just haven't worked out how to share them - and this stifles their effectiveness.

So, what's *your* message?

Key point

Messages are the doorway to your ideas. They bring information to life. Yet most speakers don't kown what their message is! The main reason is they're too close to the subject. We call this the Closeness Problem (and that's the next principle...).

PRINCIPLE 3: WE ALL HAVE THE CLOSENESS PROBLEM

Has someone ever given you directions and used these words '...*you can't miss it!*' (we all have).

But can you miss it? Usually, the answer is yes. Easily and often.

This disconnect between the giver and the receiver of directions occurs because the giver has a clear and complete *picture* of all the surroundings, yet their words don't convey their full understanding. So there is a gap between what the giver knows and what the receiver hears.

This classic cartoon from 1976 shows a cop, who lives in a town, giving directions to someone from out of town. So, he's a subject matter expert, speaking to someone who doesn't know as much about the subject. This is a bit like a business presentation, where a subject matter expert is speaking to an audience that craves clear information. When you speak in public, aren't you usually the 'subject matter expert' speaking to those who are interested in the subject? So, as you read the story below, see if you notice the similarity to many business presentations.

Imagine this. You're in a new town and need to find the cafe you've agreed to meet your friend at. You seek help from a local police officer.

"Go straight." He points. "At the lights, turn left. Walk until you see a **red building**. Go right, walk a little way and the cafe is **just around the corner**. *You can't miss it.*"

You thank him and head off, taking the first left at the lights. Heading down the next street, though, you realise there are a number of buildings that could be called 'red'. You go right after the *reddest* building.

As you look ahead, you see a couple of lanes intersecting with this road, and cafes on, or close to, every corner. Uhm, *which corner* was he referring to? (Think about it, whenever you're standing on a corner, there's usually another corner close by, isn't there?). And what did he mean by 'just around' the corner - 5 steps around the corner or 50 steps? Mmm, maybe you *can* miss it after all.

The closer we are to an issue, the harder it becomes to see the perspective of someone else

The police officer has the *closeness problem*. Actually, we all have the Closeness Problem. That is; the closer we are to an issue - the more experience we have, the more we care, the more research we've done about it - the harder it becomes to see the perspective of someone else.

In the police officer's mind, a bunch of details were 'obvious' to him but that turned out to be not so obvious to you. He delivered his message with what he *believed* was clarity ... but it wasn't clear to his audience.

Now imagine we asked him how his 'presentation' went, based on the traditional performance view of public speaking.

"It was perfect. Flawless!", he might say. *"I spoke with confidence, didn't forget anything, had good eye contact, no ums, no mistakes, had open gestures and strong body language."*

But, none of those traditional measures help our out-of-town mate reach his destination. So, what do we care about...? Message transfer!

Lack of awareness about the closeness problem is one of the biggest problems with speeches and presentations today. It's the reason most speakers don't deliver a vivid message to their audience. They think it's clear, but it's not. They assume their listeners will get the obvious point, but they don't.

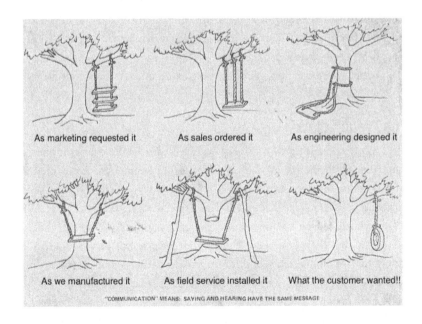

Acknowledgement: T and W Fleet

* The famous 'Tree Swing Pictures' (above) have been around since the 1960s and now come in several variations. They illustrate the challenges of seeing the world from just one perspective.

The expert's dilemma

The closeness problem is one of the biggest hurdles we face as we try to construct that holy grail: *a clear, easily recalled, transferable message.* Whether it's our local knowledge, the expertise we have around our job, or the perspective we have from our position in the organisation, we all have a blind spot that makes it very difficult to separate what *we* know from what *others* know. We can't 'see the wood for the trees'.

Put another way, the longer you have known something, the more difficult it becomes to remember what it was like *not to know* it. We need to be better at looking at the world from the audience's perspective.

Look at the problems this causes. According to a Louis Harris study, 'less than a third of employees say that management provides clear goals and directions'. However, in a Forum Corporation survey of Fortune 500 *executives*, 82 per cent believed that 'everyone who needs to know' understood their corporate strategy.

In other words, leaders think that everyone understands their message, but they don't.

"They're all idiots"

I did some consulting work for a sales director who was complaining about the performance of his merchandising team. We were chatting about the idea of 'once we know something, we forget what it was like *not* to know it'. Then his face changed. The penny dropped.

"I now realise that we just *assume* our merchandisers will get it," he said. "We forget that they don't have the training, experience or exposure to the product that we do. So when they don't get it, we call them lazy. The reality is that the fault lies with us. We haven't made it clear enough for them."

The great thing about this was that *by seeing the world from the listener's perspective,* the sales director was well on the way to solving his problem. It was now simple to design training based on his new perspective.

Your ability to craft a vivid message depends a lot on learning to step into the shoes of others. Oh, and by the way, if you think the closeness problem doesn't affect you, *then you probably have it worse than most.* The reality is that misunderstandings are normal. That's right, normal.

All words are vague

There is an interesting little book called *Why Didn't You Say That in the First Place?* by Richard Heyman. He outlines a field of research called ethnomethodology – the study of people's methods for making sense of each other using language.

The key finding of their research is that misunderstandings are normal. Commonplace. We should *expect* them. If you don't expect ambiguous communication and have the skills to manage it, your life will be frustrating, and you won't even recognise the cause.

For example, in a fist thumping speech, a CEO urges his staff to improve 'service'.

> *He says, "This company is built on service and will continue to thrive if we all focus on service. Is that clear? Now, I think everyone knows what they need to do to improve service, so go out and do it!"*

What happened next? No one was quite sure what to do, but the heads of marketing and sales started arguing for more money to add people and technology, thinking they had approval from the CEO to spend like drunken sailors, because that's the way they perceived they would improve 'service'. But the CEO didn't want to add staff or increase budget, he thought he was simply asking for a change in attitude. This led to misunderstandings, wasted effort and ultimately great frustration.

Almost any word can be interpreted multiple ways - 'Leadership'; 'Quality'; 'Productivity'; 'Value'. All of these can have different meanings across different departments and up and down the levels of a single company, let alone across different organisations.

How much do you love jargon?

Then of course there is jargon. Consider the following line from a radio executive pitching to an advertising agency:

> *"Get on board with us because there is great synergy with your market, and our creative and resources will give you great cut through."*

The words 'synergy', 'creative' and 'cut-through' are jargon. By asking a couple of clarifying questions his message became:

> "By committing to this six month proposal, you will reach more of your potential market than with any other media. Our creative team has devised a campaign to position your product as the number one choice to your tightly defined audience."

This statement now uses more specific language where there is less chance the words would be misinterpreted. Consider the difference between the words 'creative' and 'creative team'. The first term, 'creative' could mean 1) the ads we produce, 2) the team that produces them, 3) our general creative vibe.

However, 'creative team' can only mean one thing, so it sticks in the mind of the audience.

Can you identify a term used in your industry or organisation, that could be interpreted in multiple ways? Or a word that you couldn't really explain that well if someone said 'What does 'X' really mean?'.

Become a great translator

While on holiday a few years ago I met Bill, who made his fortune building aquariums - big, commercial aquariums, worth millions of dollars, of the type you see at hotels in Dubai. When I asked him what his role was he said, "Basically, I'm a translator".

He shared a story about a meeting with a client and one of his technical people. The client had a vision for their aquarium - it would look fantastic, which would draw in the crowds. The technician knew the limitations of what could be done. Bill knew his job in the meeting would probably be to *translate*. The meeting went along these lines:

Client:	*"We want the sharks swimming in a tube over the top of the customers. This will look spectacular."*
Technician:	*"There are limitations to what can be done. It's an issue of fluid dynamics. There needs to be sufficient water volume ..." (he goes on with more technical stuff).*
Client:	*"Hey, we have $25 million to spend. We want the sharks in a tube."*
Technician:	*"But the technical limitations, the fluid dynamics..."*
Client:	*"Just do it!"*
Bill:	*"If we build it like that **the sharks will die**."*
Client:	*Pause. "Oh. I see... What do you recommend?"*

This story is a classic case of the closeness problem. The technician could only see the technical perspective, while the client could only see the marketing perspective. Think about the value Bill added by being a translator.

This is the value you can add as a presenter. Look into the mind of your listener and 'translate' the information so they see the value you see - to ensure they *get it*.

Key points

We all have the closeness problem. To overcome it, you need to see yourself as someone who will translate that information into clear, tight messages. How?

- By imagining yourself in the audience's shoes;
- By removing any terminology that the audience might find vague;
- By making sure your message is not lost in a sea of data.

PRINCIPLE 4: YOUR NATURAL STYLE IS THE RIGHT STYLE

You might be thinking; with all this talk about *messages*, aren't we forgetting about **connecting with the audience**? Don't I need to engage my listeners all the way through the talk? Good question. Yes, that is important. And relaxing into your natural style is a great way to connect with them.

About 20 years ago, I spoke at my first corporate conference. I was working for the biggest radio broadcaster in the country in a sales and marketing role. I had only been with them for six months and saw this as a chance to make a mark. It was a big deal to me.

I had two talks to give. The first was the formal presentation, focusing on sales and marketing strategies. The second talk was 'off the agenda' – I'd shared an idea with my manager some weeks earlier and she suggested I explain the idea to the group at the conference.

Just before the conference a few of us were offered the chance to attend a presentation skills training course. I eagerly raised my hand. I wanted to be a confident and compelling speaker and I wasn't there yet!

Anxiety increased after the training!

Unfortunately the course did more harm than good. I became more self conscious and more nervous after the course.

As the conference got closer I diligently prepared my formal talk, trying to incorporate all the public speaking tips I had been taught. I worked hard. I practiced over and over, trying to control the gestures that the course told me were 'way too frequent'. I worked hard to make sure I followed the presentation rules 'just right'.

In spite of the huge amount of effort I put in, my speech didn't go well. As soon as I stood up I felt stiff, uncomfortable and inadequate. My anxiety levels started off high and got worse. I felt tremendous pressure to deliver something *dramatic*, yet I constantly felt I was forgetting some of the tips, that I wasn't following the rules perfectly. The harder I tried and the more effort I squandered to 'add impact' the more disconnected I felt. It was a train wreck.

Trying to remember all the rules - what to do with my hands, how fast to speak, how often to pause, and so on, cluttered my mind. I felt pulled in different directions. With all the mental noise going on in my head, I just felt lost. It was exhausting. I don't remember exactly what I said, but people weren't even polite. They were clearly bored. I came away from that first presentation beating myself up about all the things I'd done wrong.

Then a funny thing happened when it was time for the second presentation.

I'd done a lot less preparation and no rehearsal at all. I figured this one was just about *explaining my idea* – there was no dramatic effort or formality required. It was just going to be a chat.

The idea was clear in my mind and I simply shared it with the audience, in the same way I had shared it with my manager. I ended with a short summary (message) and suggested next steps - because it made sense to do so.

It was easy.

The audience loved it when I didn't try so hard!

Following this second presentation I was surprised to receive positive feedback. My manager was impressed and thanked me for the idea. People were engaged! A few commented on how much more relaxed I looked and sounded, compared with my first speech. And everyone I spoke to was able to restate my idea – *they got the message.*

The big difference was that my focus was on *helping the audience understand the idea and it's value,* not worrying about what my hands or body were doing. My body and voice simply followed my clarity and belief in the idea.

Looking back, I can see how damaging the traditional public speaking approach had been. I'd done all that training and practice for what? An incoherent speech in which I had felt incredibly nervous and uncomfortable. Yet, when I **ignored all the rules** and just talked to my audience during the second talk, I'd managed to get my point across very clearly. And it was effortless.

Later, I talked to my colleagues who also attended presentation skills training, and found that about half of them felt just as I did - that the course had made them *more* anxious and far more self conscious. It was becoming clear that a lot of public speaking training was shallow, contradictory and impractical. People were wasting energy going in the wrong direction.

Natural style unlocks your talent

Remember, uncertainty is the cause of anxiety (Principle 1). Well, a lot of uncertainty is generated when we believe we have to change who we are, in order to speak in front of a group. Think about it. What if you could be yourself when public speaking? Wouldn't that reduce uncertainty and require much less effort? Wouldn't that help you to think clearly on stage?

Ah, but what will the audience think? Don't they expect a good speaker to act a certain way? Nuh. They don't. When you radiate your natural style, you are more credible. You are seen as more sincere, trustworthy. You communicate with less effort and think with more clarity.

And guess what? When you're relaxed in your own skin, it helps people around you relax as well. As French philosopher Blaise Pascal put it:

> *"When we encounter a natural style we are always surprised and delighted, for we thought to see a speaker² and found a person."*

The problem with rules

Imagine you're about to make a big presentation and your manager (let's call him Mr Rules-I've-Heard) decides to give you a last minute pep talk. Here's Mr Rules-I've-Heard's attempt to share his wisdom with you:

> *"Body language is everything, so don't slouch. Use open gestures and a lot of facial expressions and don't turn your back on the audience - or put your hands in your pockets.*

It's not what you say that matters, it's mainly about your non-verbal communication and the visual look. Gee, I wish you'd worn a power tie. Anyway, remember to smile, think positive and get off to a strong start because first impressions are everything! If you make a bad first impression you won't be able to recover. Try to have some authority in your voice like JFK or Winston Churchill or Martin Luther King and definitely don't say 'um' or 'ah'. We've gone to great effort to get the slides professionally designed so everything else up there will look perfect. I'm sorry you didn't get much of a chance to go through the slides, but they just came back from the graphics department. Now remember, don't look at your notes – it's unprofessional. Never walk in front of the screen. And by the way, if you feel nervous, take a moment to visualise everything going well – and if that doesn't work imagine the audience naked. Now, go and knock 'em dead!"

Does this advice make you feel like you can relax and be yourself in front of an audience? Have you heard some of these gems in the past? It's probably a bit over the top as an example, because we don't tend to hear all these rules in one go. They are absorbed bit by bit from a range of people, books and courses, over time.

But the result is the same. Confusion, overwhelm and the implication that public speaking is a mysterious black art that is disconnected from the real world. This advice is not the foundation for a relaxed and natural talk. And do you notice there's not one comment in all that about the most important thing of all - the message that needs to be transferred. That's quite typical too.

Rules stop you connecting with your listeners

The best way to connect with your audience is to be genuine. We are more effective when we *reduce* the barriers between us and our audience, not increase them with a forced style.

Performance rules can be a problem because, by definition, a rule says, ***don't think!*** *Don't trust your own judgement, don't assess each situation on its own merits, just follow this rule...every time.* It suggests there is a single 'right' way of presenting and that any deviation from this way is 'wrong'. In other words, *you* are wrong if you don't fit the 'optimum' style. This leads to 'cookie-cutter' speakers or 'clones', as one of our clients recently described the people coming back from a previous training course.

A rule I was taught years ago was that you should make 6 gestures per minute. Not 5, not 7 – 6. But I average about 60 gestures a minute, so the implication is that my natural style was 10 times wrong!

By the way, American psychologist David McNeill, in his book *Hand and Mind*, suggests that gestures are a natural part of an individual's thought process. Trying to stop them or control them interrupts your mental flow. He also says there is no point trying to force gestures into some arbitrary rule because they are 'not subject to a system of standards'. In other words, *the best thinking comes when you gesture in a way that is natural to you.*

Think guidelines, not rules

In the movie *Ghostbusters*, Sigourney Weaver plays a woman who is possessed by a demon who attempts to seduce Bill Murray's character. He says;

> *"I make it a rule never to get involved with possessed people."*
>
> *(She kisses him passionately and continues to seduce him.)*
>
> *"Actually, it's more of a guideline than a rule..."*

His switch illustrates the added flexibility associated with guidelines. Rules are fixed, whereas guidelines can give clear direction while allowing for modification. Rules are terrific for machines and rigid hierarchical systems where things need to be identical no matter where or when they are used, but attempting to make all human presenters identical doesn't work.

Here's a story from my teenage years that illustrates the value of guidelines over rules. When I headed out to a party my dad didn't lay down a long list of rules for me. There was no lecture about not taking drugs or drinking alcohol, not smoking, not stealing or damaging other people's property, etc, etc. In fact, it would be difficult to come up with enough rules to cover every situation one might face.

Instead, he left me with a single guideline. As I ventured out the door to face the temptations of the world, he simply said,

'Be a gentleman.'

At the time I thought it was an old-fashioned, boring comment from my out-of-touch dad. In hindsight I recognise the wisdom in my father's approach.

Guidelines apply to any situation

That guideline was more valuable than a set of rules because it was flexible enough to apply to *any* situation. His message would pop into my head as I faced various choices and (most of the time) I was able to make good decisions. Rather than mindlessly following (or rebelling against) the rules I was given, his guideline meant that I ended up using my own judgements and making my own decisions. It helped build the muscle of thinking for myself.

Now, I'm not a parenting expert and rules can certainly be valuable when you identify that a child is too young to use their own judgement, but when it comes to human-to-human communication, rules shut down your thinking, while guidelines help activate your awareness.

So, a more productive way to think about the *rules* of presenting is treat them as guidelines.

What's the difference? A rule says 'don't think, just do', and a guideline says, 'Here's a proven path, but use your own judgement for each situation'.

- Guidelines give you more freedom to clarify and deliver your ideas in a way that feels natural to you.
- Guidelines give you direction, whereas rules lock you in a box.
- Guidelines take into account the variation in style between one person and the next, whereas rules assume everyone is the same.
- Guidelines encourage natural style, rules stifle it.
- Rules clutter your mind; guidelines let you focus on getting your message across.
- Rules wake you up to give you a sleeping pill. Guidelines let you sleep.

Most of the apparently rigid dos and don'ts of speaking should be reinterpreted as guidelines.

Here are a few examples:

Rule	Guideline
You should have exactly 3 seconds of eye contact with each person in your audience.	Eye contact is important to engage the audience – try to catch people's eyes regularly.
Don't put your hands in your pockets	Putting your hands in your pockets generally looks informal. Decide for yourself whether it matters for a particular audience.
You must follow a particular structure (e.g, you *must* have three points)	Structure helps the audience understand your information – choose a structure that brings your message to life.
You should have six gestures per minute and they should be below shoulder height, but above the waist. The three parts of a good gesture are: 1) the entry, 2) the stroke, 3) the return to a resting position.	Gestures can be effective at enhancing spoken communication. Some people gesture a lot, others don't. When you are comfortable, gestures tend to flow with the ideas that you're presenting. Let them.

How to find your natural style

Make up your own mind about the 'presentation rules'. Watch successful speakers doing their stuff. You'll notice they have different styles, regularly break the 'rules', yet look comfortable in their own skin.

You don't really need a list of steps to find your natural style. Just be the style that helps you think clearly and pursue the pace that helps you breathe comfortably.

Natural Style examples

Richard Branson and Bill Gates say 'um' a lot when they speak. Jack

Welch gets angry. Bill Clinton sometimes has long pauses and Al Gore is wooden. Who cares? We accept them rough edges and all.

Microsoft was built by 2 men with opposite styles. Bill Gates' introvert-style with a slow rate of speech and little animation. And Steven Ballmer with a table-thumping, jump-around-the-stage extrovert style.

Steve Jobs was almost laid back when he spoke. Sheryl Sandberg, Facebook's COO is animated when she speaks, Meg Whitman, CEO of Hewlett Packard is less so. On TV, Oprah screams and waves her arms in the air while Ellen is funny and engaging without as much animation.

On the public speaking circuit, Tom Peters and Tony Robbins are super-energetic extrovert-style speakers, while Deepak Chopra and Stephen Covey (who died recently after 25 years as one of the world's most in-demand and highly paid speakers) have a low-key introvert style.

Richard Dawkins' style is stiff and condescending, but his explanations and message are extremely clear. Eckhart Tolle has a soft, mousey voice and long pauses, but captures audiences with beautiful explanations, memorable stories and quotable one-liners.

Should we teach Stephen Hawking body language?

Stephen Hawking speaks via an annoying computer generated voice, but his TED talk has 7 million views. Yet he has NO STYLE. He can't move. Who would like to lecture Stephen Hawking on body language?

The common denominator of effective speakers is not style, it's the clarity of their ideas and the certainty with which they deliver them. Focus on explaining your ideas. You won't please all the people all the time, but your best chance of success will come from delivering great explanations, in *your natural style*.

Key points

Ahhh... What a load off your shoulders! You don't have to be perfect. You don't have to compare your style to others. Find a way to relax and be yourself. People will accept your rough edges (as long as you provide clear messages and useful explanations).

---

[2] Okay – Pascal actually said 'writer', not 'speaker', but the point is just as relevant.

PRINCIPLE 5: YOU CAN CONTROL ANXIETY BY UNDERSTANDING IT

This is a picture of me after smashing my head on a skate ramp. Can you see the black eye and 5 stitches? I went to the Riverside skate park during a mid-life crisis moment in my early 40s. Decided I was gonna learn to ride the half-pipe. Why? Because I'm not too old for that! And I'll probably look really cool...

The half-pipe won...

So without any practise on these kinds of ramps I rolled towards the edge. I don't remember the details from that point, because, as you may have heard, when a person is knocked unconscious the mind often erases the memory of the event. But I know from my injuries and the explanations from the kids who peeled me off the concrete, that my legs flew out from under me and my head smashed on the top edge of the metal and concrete ramp, knocking me out instantly.

I slid down the ramp, unconscious, like a sack of meat, coming to rest at the bottom, face down. They told me I was 'out' for about 2 mins. When I came to, I wondered what the sticky stuff was on my hands, chest, and face (turns out it was blood), and why a bunch of 15 year old kids were standing over me.

As I lifted my head, one of my new skate buddies said, "Are you all right mister?" I thought about that question for a few seconds, oriented myself, and thankfully realised I was ok. By the way, when they told me I'd been face down for 2 minutes I wondered what these kids were doing all that time. I imagined 1 or 2 of them gently kicking my lifeless body and saying, "I reckon this old man's dead!"

Anyway, I got to my feet ok, but had a gash above my left eye that was bleeding profusely. Then, a cute thing happened. Some of the kids shared their injury stories with me. "Don't worry about it mate, we've all crashed. I just got the pins out of my arm" said one. For a moment I felt some satisfaction. My mid-life goal was complete. I was one of the dudes! Hanging with the cool kids. (Actually I was bleeding all over the feet of the cool kids.)

Then someone's mum came over to check my wound and said, "You're gonna need some stitches, Luv. Better get off to the hospital". I responded in a sheepish, childlike tone. "Right. Yeah, Good Idea." I didn't feel that cool anymore.

Nerve damage? Brain damage?

I came back to reality and headed to the nearest hospital to get my eye stitched. As I was sitting, waiting to be treated, my left arm started to shake. Then my head started twitching like a coked-up zombie. This shaking escalated, uncontrollably, increasing and decreasing in waves like a Geiger counter until my whole body was shaking.

'What have I done to myself', I thought. 'Brain damage? Nerve damage? What an idiot! How could I let this happen?' My internal voice, *critiquing my past actions* and *worrying about my future*, got louder and louder. It was, quite frankly, freaking me out.

I stood up and zombie-twisted my way over to the reception desk. "Excuse me," I said to the guy at the desk. He looked up from what he was doing and noticed my gyrations. "This shaking you're doing..." he said, pointing at me. "Is that normal for you?"

"Ahh, no mate! That's what I wanted to talk to you about. I don't feel right!"

He called a nurse over. She asked me a series of questions, twice, and finally said I had nothing to worry about. "It's called *shock*" she said. "Massive amounts of adrenaline are being released in your body as a result of the physical trauma. Are you cold?"

I wasn't cold.

"You'll be fine," she reassured.

Cause and effect

The shaking was a physical symptom of adrenaline, so I could see **the cause was temporary** and that the **physical symptom** would soon fade. I knew a bit about the impact of too much adrenaline, so what she said made perfect sense.

I sat down. And had an epiphany!

The extreme shaking didn't stop, but I noticed my mind was completely calm. It was then I recognised a *distinct separation* between the physical symptoms (caused by adrenaline in this case) and the ability to think calmly.

The explanation by the nurse made sense and gave me *certainty* about what was going on in my body. It was now much easier to separate my physical symptoms from my *mental response* to those symptoms.

And you can too.

I've taught thousands of people to recognise this separation between the physical symptoms of anxiety and their mental response to those symptoms. They've learned how to strengthen their ability to think clearly under pressure - no matter how strong the symptoms may be.

Understanding the stress response

The reason for sharing the skate park story isn't to warn overconfident early middle-aged wannabes about the perils of the half-pipe. It's to share the realities of the stress response, which can be quite similar in a public speaking situation as it was in that emergency room.

Like a thermostat, the stress response kicks in when you need to be 'on'. It works in recognisable ways whether you need to be 'on' because you're in physical danger, or because you're in front of an audience and want your presentation to go well.

The intensity of the physical symptoms vary from person to person, and are influenced by things like:

- The importance of the situation to you.
- How much sleep you've had.
- What you've eaten (e.g., caffeine can add to the adrenaline rush).
- Your emotional state.
- Genetic differences.

Even with these variables, the stress response is pretty easy to understand.

Firstly, let's look at the brain in a simplified way. Think of the brain as just having 2 parts - top and bottom. The 'top' is the neocortex ('new' brain) which is where all that conscious thinking takes place: reasoning and logic. This is what humans have over animals - a larger neocortex.

The 'bottom' part of the brain is more *instinctive* and emotional. This part of the brain doesn't 'think' so much as 'react'.

The stress response kicks in automatically

Guess which part of the brain controls the stress response? The part that can think, or the part that *can't* think? The answer is the latter: The stress response is controlled by the part of our brain that *can't* think. The instinctive part. The reptile part.

Now, you might be wondering if giving control of the stress response to the unconscious part of the brain was a bad idea. The physical symptoms of the stress response can seem overwhelming or even debilitating, so why have the reactionary part of the brain take responsibility for it?

One reason. *Speed.*

When we came across a sabre-tooth tiger at the time of cavemen, we didn't waste precious seconds processing the potential threat and consciously deciding to prime our bodies to deal with the danger. Instead, the 'fight-or-flight' response kicked in so we were instantly ready to fight or flee.

So, whether you're face-to-face with a sabre-tooth or the board of directors, the primitive part of your brain is attempting to *prime you for your 'important event'*. You might see these symptoms as a distraction, but the stress response is simply trying to prepare you to deal with important events. And the symptoms can be easy to understand and manage. Let's break it down. The stress response is built on 2 things:

1. Adrenaline release

The adrenal glands sit on top of the kidneys and are quite small. About the size of a walnut and weighing less than a grape, they pack a powerful punch when they release adrenaline to give you energy. However, since we're not fighting or fleeing, the surplus adrenaline energy leads to physical symptoms like: increased heart rate, sweating, blushing, shaking, feeling sick to the stomach, dry mouth, and so on. It can also cause us to speed up our rate of speech. Do you recognise any of these symptoms from public speaking anxiety?

2. Muscle contraction

The second thing the stress response does is contract your muscles (so you're ready to fight, or run away from, that tiger). The physical symptoms from this include tightness in the throat (have you noticed how a lot of people need to clear their throat or drink water at the start of a talk? Muscle tightness is the reason), and shallow breathing.

Try this now - flex your stomach and chest. Now take a deep breath while they're flexed. How much air do you get? With contracted muscles, we tend to get only 10%-50% of the air in our lungs compared to normal breathing. As a result, most people are not breathing comfortably when they speak in public. And not getting the normal amount of oxygen can make us feel more out of control.

So the physical symptoms associated with public speaking anxiety can be understood. They're not dark forces attacking you. They can be traced back to the 2 components of the stress response; adrenaline and contracting muscles.

Even though these symptoms are triggered automatically, when you understand them, it is possible to 'release' some of them *simply by acknowledging their existence*. At minimum, your increased awareness reduces their intensity.

In fact, the intensity of your anxiety can fit on a scale from 1 to 10. Anxiety at the level of 2, 3 or 4 on the scale is manageable. You feel it, but you're able to think clearly enough to achieve your speaking goals.

But letting your mind run wild can take you up to 9 or 10 (11?) on the scale, and at that level, your mind and body are in a loop.

How you think about your symptoms, determines their intensity

Let's take the example of your hand shaking. We now know why this happens. It's the direct result of adrenaline. The *reality* is, your hand is shaking. We can't get away from that fact. However, there are now 2 ways for you to think about that fact. The rational way goes something like this:

> *"Ok, my hand is shaking. But I know why. The adrenaline released by my brain is giving me more energy. Thanks brain! It's a little distracting, but it's natural and it doesn't stop me getting my message across. I'll focus my attention on something more important."*

From here, the shaking settles down, or at least doesn't get worse. It might stay at a 3 or 4 out of 10 intensity, but now that there's no drama associated with it, it doesn't stop you getting your message across and engaging your audience.

Here's how the mind will think about it when it's full of uncertainty and unaware why the symptoms occur:

> *"Oh God, my hand is shaking, and I'm about to speak to the Board of Directors. I'm losing control of my body! That can't be good!!"*

Now you hear the echo of uncertain thoughts like, 'I'm losing control' and 'What's happening to me!'or 'What if the shaking gets worse?'. This high-drama thinking increases uncertainty which is the fundamental cause of anxiety. So what happens next? Your hand shakes even more and before long you're in a mental loop that can overwhelm your senses.

The mental loop goes something like this: Your heart pounds and you think, 'Crikey, my heart's pounding, that's not good!' Your panic adds more fear and uncertainty. So your heart pounds more and you think, 'Crikey, my heart's pounding *more*, that's *really* not good!!'. And so on. A mental loop.

Do you still get nervous, Cam?

Public speaking anxiety is often ranked as the 'number 1 fear' on the List of Lists, yet many of us think that we are the only ones who get so nervous. I've worked with sportspeople, actors, musicians, politicians, CEOs, writers, TV hosts and more. All feel nervous ahead of 'doing their thing' on an important 'stage'.

I'm often asked if I still get nervous in front of an audience. The short answer is, not really, but geez I used to suffer badly. That's one of the reasons I teach this stuff. I needed to learn it myself.

The full answer is that I get nervous a bit, sometimes. It depends on the amount of uncertainty associated with an event. Trying new things still triggers the stress response. When I did my first 5-minute standup comedy routine I was nervous. It was new to me. The crowd was more aggressive than a corporate conference. And I wasn't used to the dark room and the blinding lights in my eyes. But I felt prepared, committed to my jokes and it went ok.

The last time I felt my heart pumping out of my chest and my face blushing hot was when I didn't follow my own advice. I walked into a difficult room with *layer upon layer* of uncertainty leading up to the event.

Here's what happened. A few years ago I was asked to speak at a Canberra conference for government economists, however I was unable to get a clear brief of what was expected or what the theme of the conference was. It was booked at the last minute by someone's assistant who said, 'All I know is they want you to speak from 2pm-3pm'. Normally I would find the person who put the conference together, ask about the audience, the other speakers, the outcomes they were trying to achieve, and so on. But in this case I wasn't able to get that background information.

Layers of uncertainty

This was the **first layer of uncertainty**.

The largest amount of uncertainty was generated from the fact that I made the mistake of thinking that I had to be different to my normal self. The audience was filled with government ministers and senior economists. I imagined that I needed to be more serious than usual - more intellectual, more sombre. (I was wrong by the way. It turned out they were just people - who had the same public speaking challenges as the rest of us.)

There was more. My flight, on the morning of the event, was delayed twice. Normally I fly in the day before an event to ensure this doesn't happen. But this gig was full of last minute decisions. For 3 hours leading up to my presentation, I wasn't sure I would get there on time.

This was **another layer of uncertainty**.

I arrived with a few minutes to spare. Phew! The person who was supposed to meet me wasn't there. No big deal. That happens. I found another organiser-person and asked if I could get into the room to set up and test the equipment.

"Oh no. They're still finishing off a session", she said. "And there is no break, you need to start as soon as he finishes, but you're not allowed to go in until he comes out." "Really?!" I said.

When they finally let me in, I walked in from the back of the room, past 80 bored-looking faces and spent 10 minutes fighting computer equipment that didn't work. My mind was screaming unresolved thoughts like: 'Should I chat to them now, while I'm setting up? Or just smile and focus on what I'm doing. Crikey, they look so bored. And so serious! Hey, I'll blame the organisers for the disorganisation. Nah, that will probably make me look worse...'. And so on.

I was hot, my cheeks were red, my heart was pounding and I felt acid-like anxiety throughout my body. But even though it was uncomfortable, after 10 minutes, we got the technology working. I apologised for the delay and got on with the presentation. From that point on, it went as planned and the anxiety subsided after a few minutes. I even got a smile out of the audience.

Even with these physical symptoms, I was able to think reasonably clearly, not placing too much emphasis on the mental chatter. I focused on that which I could control. So it didn't have the drama, shame or pain I used to experience.

It drained my energy at the time, but I saw the stress as temporary. It happened. I did my best (which was received well). I learned something from the experience and moved onto the next thing. Some people hold on to the emotion of presentation disasters for years. The trick is to release the emotion of unpleasant speaking events and focus on what we can learn from them for next time.

So there's my story. Hope it helps.

The solution: Redirect your attention

Now, you might be thinking; 'Cam, it's easy to say 'don't panic' but harder to do in real life'. Sure, that's true. But it's really just a matter of awareness and a bit of practice. The secret is to *flip your thinking* from unconscious reactions, to conscious management of the situation. How? First, become aware of what's happening, and second redirect your attention to escape the mental loop.

Redirecting your attention won't magically eliminate all your anxiety. But it will stop you from getting caught in a loop that's out of your control.

So where do you redirect your attention? It can be something physical, like breathing, grounding your feet on the earth, pausing or releasing the tension in your shoulders. Or you can focus your attention on an idea, such as 'All I need to do is help them understand this subject", or 'They want me to succeed because it will help them', or 'I can only do my best so there's no point worrying about anything now that I'm here'.

I encourage my clients to find their own area to direct their attention because everybody's different. However, I've found that the most universally effective place to direct your attention is your breathing.

Are you breathing comfortably when you speak? Most people are not.

Breathing *comfortably* can regulate both your mind and body. So if you're not sure where to redirect your attention, this is the place to start. However, be careful about listening to that annoying voice in your head that says,

> *'You haven't got time to slow down and breathe comfortably!*
> *They're all looking at you. Hurry up!'*

Ignore this voice if it shows up. You have plenty of time. You could probably speak at *half* the pace you currently do and it would not seem strange to the audience if you were speaking with certainty.

Some people ask, 'What's the optimum pace to speak? How many words per minute?' There is no universal answer to this question. Everybody is different. But I know one thing. The right pace for *you* is the pace where you're able to breathe comfortably.

Redirect your attention to finding the pace that works for *you* and you'll find that a lot of your anxiety just dissolves (in combination with the other suggestions in this book).

Key points

Nerves are normal. The stress response is not only normal, but healthy. It focuses our attention and gives us the energy needed to do a good job. Peace of mind comes from 1) turning down the volume of the unconscious chatter by understanding what's happening, and 2) thinking clearly about your situation and redirecting your attention.

This includes getting clear on your message and structure. Hey! That's what we're going to cover next.

VIVID METHOD PART TWO: CREATE A SPEECH OUTLINE

"**If you want to teach people a new way of thinking, don't bother trying to teach them. Instead, give them a tool, the use of which will lead to new ways of thinking.**"

- **Buckminster Fuller**

WHAT IS A SPEECH OUTLINE?

A Vivid Speech Outline guides you through the refinement of 2 things:

1. Message

2. Structure

You clarify your message first, which then guides your thinking as you structure your ideas. But before we go into the step-by-step creation of a speech outline, let's look at the experiences some people have during the *planning stage* of a speech or presentation.

Do you have a preferred procrastination schedule?

Can you relate to the following story? You get an email from your boss asking you to deliver a 30-minute speech in a fortnight? No worries, you reply. 2 weeks. That's plenty of time. You add the speech to your to do list and forget about it for a while.

A week goes by. You feel a faint pang of anxiety – or is it guilt? – as you realise you probably should have made a start already. *I'll get to it today.* But it was a busy day! You put it off until tomorrow.

This continues until it's 1 day to go and adrenaline is driving you. You work on your presentation all day, but without a method or structure to guide you, it's difficult to feel certain that your preparation is complete.

Time is up.

Here is the crucial question as you finish your preparation: Which of these 2 thoughts goes through your mind?

'Great. That's clear. I feel ready!'

Or...

'Agh. That will have to do. I'm out of time.'

Unfortunately, the thought, *'that will have to do, I'm out of time'* can leave you with a feeling of incompletion and uncertainty. This, in turn, can have a diabolical impact on physical and mental energy levels *during* your talk. When you stand in front of your audience, do you experience the residue of uncertainty about your preparation, or do you have a feeling of completeness and clarity that takes you by the hand and effortlessly guides you through the presentation?

Typical procrastination schedule

6 days to go:
Not sure where to start. No reliable method to prepare. Put it off until tomorrow. (Anxiety level: happily avoiding.)

5 days to go:
Gather some info. Create/copy a few PowerPoint slides. Can finish them later. You wake in the early hours with a mixture of good ideas for your talk, and self-criticism for not being ready yet. A little progress. (Anxiety level: a slight hum.)

4 days to go:
Busy day! No time. For a moment you wonder whether you allowed yourself to be lost in busy-work as a way of avoiding the speech. Nah, you're just a busy person. (Anxiety level: Starting to build.)

3 days to go:
You think; 'I should have prepared yesterday'. Guilt now added to the mix. Spend some time arranging slides and formatting. The voice in your head is giving you a hard time. 'Am I really up to this? Will I come across as an impostor when I'm supposed to be the expert? Can I get someone else to do it?' (Anxiety level: What's that strange feeling in your gut?)

2 days to go:
A few hours preparing, but you're tired from the sleepless nights and your shoulders are heavy with the burden of incompletion. Feeling somewhat drained and frustrated. (Anxiety level: Difficult to get to sleep.)

1 day to go:
Rehearsing while physically and mentally exhausted. Finish preparing with the thought 'That will *have* to do, I'm out of time'. (Anxiety level: Why does my skin hurt?!)

Day of the presentation:
As you speak, you feel slightly depleted, with a week of mental anguish festering in your gut. (Anxiety level: High. Energy level: Drained).

Is this preparation problem simply due to a lack of discipline? Probably not. One reason people find public speaking daunting is they don't have a simple, **method to sort their thoughts**. Discipline without direction is a recipe for wasted effort and fatigue.

Without a method to focus your preparation, it's difficult to get clear about what you're going to say. No matter how much time and effort you put into it, you finish your preparation feeling uncertain.

So, what about you?

Do you have a method to prepare that you can rely on? If so, fantastic. Use it. If not, consider the Vivid Speech Outline. Over the years we examined dozens of preparation methods. We've tested and refined this one in thousands of training courses, workshops and executive coaching sessions. The Vivid Speech Outline is a way of *directing your attention* while preparing. It harnesses the ClarityFirst principles and steers them to your advantage. It saves time, reduces effort and leverages your knowledge and talent, instead of diffusing them in clutter and confusion.

Why does it work so well? The speech outline as checklist

Do you recall the 2009 crash landing of US Airways Flight 1549 in the Hudson River? The plane lost power in both engines after flying into a flock of geese, soon after leaving New York. Sometimes referred to as 'The Miracle on the Hudson', all 155 people on board survived. The cockpit audio from the 'Black box recorder' was played over and over on talk shows and newscasts.

The captain, Chesley Sullenberger, who was lauded for his skill and composure during the crisis, can be heard clearly on the cockpit audio relying on checklists during the first part of the transcript.

You can hear the pilots clearly following checklists. No matter how much experience they have, all pilots use checklists. On every single flight. Great chefs still use *recipes* to ensure their creations are repeatable. The construction industry uses *plans* and checklists to manage building projects and prevent the confusion of having different tradespeople working over the top of each other. In fact, in almost every industry, checklists of one sort or another are used to manage the demands of high volumes of information.

It just makes sense.

Yet, for some reason, few people use a reliable checklist for the creation of a speech or presentation. Maybe it has something to do with the fact that people think of an outline, as an *extra* step. 'Wouldn't I be better spending my limited time writing my speech rather than both planning it, then writing it?' they ask.

No, you wouldn't.

Recent findings in neuroscience research show that our brains become overwhelmed much more easily and more often than most people realise. This leads to weak clarification skills, sloppy planning and wasted effort.

The neuroscience also argues that we can avoid overwhelm and improve brain performance dramatically when we do the following:

- *Get things out of our heads on to paper or screen*: because there is a tight limit to the number of things that can be held in the mind and manipulated at any one time.
- *Prioritise before we take action*: because our prefrontal cortex, the clarification part of the brain, requires a lot of energy to function.
- *Create a simple framework for thinking*: because our brain becomes overwhelmed easily and this lets it focus on one step at a time.
- *See the relationship between things visually*: because it's hard to think of new ideas if they don't connect to existing ideas in some way.
- *Simplify and chunk information*: because the most powerful tool to help the brain function at its peak, is chunking.
- *Do your sorting, comparing and deep thinking in the **outline stage**, not when overwhelmed by details*: because it keeps you focused and avoids hitting 'the wall'.

A speech outline that incorporates these techniques will benefit you in 3 ways:

First, a speech outline saves you time and effort

Adding the outline step can significantly cut preparation time and effort by getting ideas out of your head and sorted. Without an outline you are using an *Information First* approach, where you dive into *all the information* related to the talk. This is common. But it's a bit like starting a trip without looking at a map of where you're going. You get moving quickly, but you're not sure which milestones are important and can waste time in locations that take you off track. You can end up going around in circles.

Using an outline is a *Clarity First* approach, where you identify your message and key points as the first step. It's like checking the directions of a trip on Google Maps before you start driving. You prioritise before you take action. It requires clear thinking in the beginning, but saves a huge amount of time and frustration throughout the journey. My estimation is that every minute spent on getting *clarity first* will save you about 20 minutes in editing and rethinking later on.

Second, a speech outline makes you more compelling

Creating a simple framework for thinking helps us consider ideas and information objectively, which leads to more lucid and persuasive explanations.

The outline works as an attention-directing tool that helps us organise ideas more effectively. Why do we need an attention-directing tool? Neuroscience tells us that the more items we have in our mind, the more our memory degrades for each item. So getting the ideas and information out of our head and into the outline helps us focus, and access our brain's full processing power.

The longer our brain works on an idea continuously, the more it becomes exhausted. Using an outline is quicker because we leave the detail until last. It helps us simplify and chunk information. This reduces *mental steps* so we can use our brain for deep thinking, and have more mental capacity left to edit and refine.

All this creates a better environment for 'Aha!' moments in which we see more clearly what will be required to influence an audience. This helps us to be perceived as a thoughtful, focused person and leverage our knowledge and talent, which in turn leads to greater success in selling ideas.

Third, a speech outline dissolves anxiety

Creating an outline as the first step in the planning process, fills the *gaps of uncertainty* that form when you accept an offer to speak in public. Specifically, you get clear about your message, key points, structure and potential questions the audience might ask. And this happens very early in your preparation.

This is HUGE.

After completing the outline (not your whole speech or all your slides, just the outline), you'll know how to *start* your talk, how you're going to *end*, and the key 'landmarks' throughout. You'll have a good feel for the flow of your talk and you'll be prepared for the tough questions.

Knowing that you know this will dissolve a truckload of uncertainty.

In fact, when you fail to get clarity about these things early in your preparation, you can unwittingly create *an environment* for unease. This speech outline, in combination with the 5 ClarityFirst principles, creates an *environment* for natural confidence.

The reason for my rant!

I know I'm ranting about 'the outline'. But it solves so many problems at their cause! Here's another example - have you ever had a boss or colleague give you feedback on your presentation after it's complete? This doesn't usually help - it's about minor points that don't matter, or big things that are too late to change.

Instead, ask for **feedback at the outline stage**.

Show your boss the outline on a single page and ask, "Here's my key message and my supporting arguments, what do you think?" Often a manager is so impressed at your clarity, they trust you to continue without their meddling, um, I mean, their help.

If there was a drug that could make your communication twice as effective in half the time, would you take it? The Vivid Speech Outline is just such a 'drug'. And the side effects are all positive! I recommend you get addicted to scribbling an outline every time you need to communicate your ideas.

The difference between a traditional outline and a Vivid Speech Outline

The Vivid Speech Outline is turbo charged - it *speeds up* the planning process and adds *power* and *control* when speaking.

It's slightly different to a traditional outline, in 3 ways.

The *first difference* is about your message. Most public speaking methods just assume you know your message and simply leave a place for a 'summary' at the end of the outline.

Not good enough. We know from Principle 3 (we all have the Closeness Problem) that most people don't clarify a compelling message. So the outline should guide you through the crafting of your message. Some traditional outlines will guide you through a 'purpose statement', or an 'objectives statement' or a 'topic sentence' or a variation on this theme.

Still not good enough. While they might help you clarify your goals for the talk, they have one major flaw. *They are not written in the words you will say to your audience.* They are written in the words you will say to yourself. For example, a purpose statement might be:

> *'I want to impress them with my experience and convince them to the support the project.'*

What words will you actually say to your audience?

However, when will your words be translated to the exact words you will say to convince your audience? Usually never. This also means you won't have a chance to **test your message out loud** - which is so helpful in refining it.

So, with a purpose statement, when you stand up to speak, you still haven't clarified the language you will use to engage your audience - which leaves you open to vagueness and uncertainty. Too many speakers get to the end of a speech or presentation and either try to summarise their message on the fly, under the pressure of the spotlight; or they repeat some of the points they've covered; or they don't summarise at all, leaving the audience to work it out for themselves.

Preparing a Vivid Speech Outline starts with your 'Message Statement'. It helps you see your message objectively and guides your preparation with laser-like focus. A Message Statement gives you certainty about where you're headed in your speech and provides you with a strong end to your presentation.

The *second difference* between a traditional speech outline and Vivid Speech Outline is related to **structure** and **key points**. A traditional outline has the following basic structure:

A Traditional Outline:

Introduction
1. First section.
Blah blah blah
Blah blah blah

2. Second section
Blah blah blah
Blah blah blah

3. Third section
Blah blah blah
Blah blah blah

Conclusion

This is a good starting point. But it doesn't take advantage of what we know about memory and recall - that people will forget 90%-98% of what you say. This is not a bad thing - just a fact. So, it makes sense to emphasise the key point for each section *during* your talk.

If we define the 2%-10% they could remember, in the planning stage, we can seed our structure with the gold that we want them to retain. Your goal should be message *recall*, and the speech outline should help ensure your audience retains your message and key points. So, at the end we change 'summary' to 'message'. And at the end of each section we add a 'key point' to summarise the section and give the audience the short, sticky point they can easily retain. Simple, but powerful.

Here's how the Vivid outline looks with these 2 additions:

A Vivid Outline:

Introduction
1. First section
Blah blah blah
Blah blah blah
Key point for section 1

2. Second section
Blah blah blah
Blah blah blah
Key point for section 2

3. Third section
Blah blah blah
Blah blah blah
Key point for section 3

Message Statement
(The exact words of a 1 or 2 sentence message that you'd like your audience to recall or repeat...)

I call this a 'chunk' structure - where the key point of each section, or chunk, is captured as a short sentence which closes that chunk. More on Chunk Structure later.

The exact words you will say

The *third difference* is that these 2 tweaks, as well the chunk headings (everything you see in **bold** above) are written in the *exact words you will say*, from the beginning of your planning. You'll soon see that tweaking the wording of these headings can make a big difference in capturing your audience's attention early on in your talk.

Notice we haven't spent any time on the body of the talk, yet if it was a real presentation, it would be starting to feel complete. We'd have the exact words for the start, the key points and the ending. This allows us to test and refine the scope of a talk quickly and effortlessly. It's *clarity first*, not information first.

These small differences between a Vivid Speech Outline and a traditional speech outline, have dramatic benefits - for both the planning and delivery of a talk.

CRAFTING YOUR MESSAGE, STEP-BY-STEP

Now, let's put an outline together.

The first step is to define your **Message Statement**, which involves asking yourself *three questions*. Let's go through those questions now.

Question 1: WHO are you talking to?

The Roman philosopher and statesman Cicero famously said: *"If you wish to persuade me, you must think my thoughts, feel my feelings, and speak my words."*

So, the first step is to consider WHO you're talking to. *Look into the mind of your listener* and view the world from their perspective. The quickest way to do this is to consider the 4 'views' of your audience.

View 1: Their role.

For example, what does their job role focus on? Consider age, personality style, gender, and so on.

View 2: Their biases.

For example, what's their likely attitude to the subject/you/your organisation? Are they sceptical or open? For example, have they bad experiences in the past - or have all experiences been wonderful? For example, how much do they know about this subject? Is it a priority? Consider the possible blocks at this point.

View 3: Their wants.

For example, what are their needs in relation to this issue? What's important to their role generally? What do they value? What achieves their goals or gets them promoted? Any KPIs linked to this subject? (For example: profit, efficiency.)

View 4: Their concerns.

For example, what objections might pop into their mind when they hear your talk? What questions or concerns might be raised? What answers will they need to convince others? (Consider the potential negatives they may have and write them down in *their* words.)

By writing 2 or 3 points under each 'view', you'll quickly build a profile of your audience. Now you may be wondering; what if there's a range of different people in my audience, with different roles and goals? Good question. This happens a lot. Firstly, prioritise. Who do you want to influence most in this audience? Direct your key points to them. Secondly, find common wants/needs/perspectives and focus on those as well.

Let's look at an example:

Imagine you're updating a Board of 12 Directors on a project that has fallen behind schedule:

- **View 1, their role**: CEO, CTO, COO and non-executive directors; have only a medium level of knowledge of your project; are time-poor and like summaries not details; technical expertise is limited.
- **View 2, their biases**: Sceptical towards the project because this is the second delay and benefits seem a long way off. Concerned the organisation's resources are being wasted on 'pipe dream' projects.
- **View 3, their wants and needs**: Profitability, both short term and long term; need to explain decisions to shareholders and the press; need to be seen to make good decisions and run the company well.
- **View 4: Their concerns and questions**: How much more will it cost? Should we scrap it? How realistic are the benefits? How realistic is your new timeline?

Question 2: WHAT do you want them to think or do?

Now answer the question: 'WHAT do I want the audience to *think* or *do* as a result of my presentation?' This is a single idea that drives your talk.

It's the heart of your message. Clear your mind of the details and isolate one thing you want the audience members to **think** or **do**.

Firstly, 'do'. Will you want your audience to **do** something as a result of your talk? For example:

> *"Use this new process."*
>
> *"Provide $20 million in funding for this project."*
>
> *"Approve this proposal."*
>
> *"Trial this product."*
>
> *"Engage us to provide ABC service."*
>
> *"Provide feedback by XYZ date".*

Secondly, 'think'. Perhaps you don't want them to do anything, you just want them to **think** something. For example:

> *"The project is on track."*
>
> *"The project is behind, but there are good reasons for this and the situation is under control."*
>
> *"This product will provide better results at a lower price."*
>
> *"The 'X' project has 3 benefits…"*
>
> *"The restructure will be disruptive at first, but will strengthen the organisation."*
>
> *"Learning this method will make you better at your job".*

Choose one thing

Of course, you may want the audience to think or do several things. The problem is that *the more you say, the less they'll retain*. Find the single most important thing you want the audience to **think** or **do**. For the example above, you might say to yourself; '*Well, I really want them to trust me and to understand the reasons for the delay and that ultimately the benefits of the project are not in jeopardy.*'

The trouble with this is that it sounds like a purpose statement we talked about earlier. It's not written in the words you will say to your audience. Using the *words you would say*, might be something like:

> *"The project is behind, but there are good reasons for this and we have them under control."*

Great. You've isolated the main point, and made a claim. This is the *first half* of your Message Statement. Let's look at the second half of your Message Statement…

Question 3: WHY would they think or do this?

Now provide supporting evidence for your claim. **List the reasons** WHY your audience will *think* or *do* what you suggest. In our example, you're telling the board that 'the project is behind but there are good reasons for this and we have them under control'…

> *"…Opportunities were identified to make the new products 50% more profitable, but taking advantage of these opportunities has slowed things down".*

This addresses a 'good reason'.

> *"…To reduce risk, we have taken a little longer to finalise the financial structure of the project; we have that now and the project is looking more valuable than it did initially".*

This addresses both a 'good reason' and gives an example of 'under control'. And below addresses 'under control' as well.

> *"…While there has been a development delay, we have been able to lock in a reliable timeline for production and are looking at a launch in October this year."*

You might have 2 WHY points, or you might find 10 WHY points. This 3rd question is a bit of a brainstorm of reasons to support the WHAT claim you made in question 2. Don't use too many though. Prioritise and choose 2, 3 or 4 supporting points. You want a tight message statement. Now, let's put it all together…

Finalising your Message Statement

Now you've answered the 3 questions - 'WHO', 'WHAT' and 'WHY'. Your Message Statement will come together by combining the 'WHAT' and 'WHY' answers. The message should be written in the exact words that you will say to your audience. This might mean that the combination of the 'WHAT' and 'WHY' answers will need to be given a bit of polish. Let's try this with our board of directors presentation example.

WHAT:

"The project is behind, but there are good reasons for this and we have them under control. For example..."

WHY:

"...Opportunities were found to make the new products 50% more profitable, but taking advantage of these opportunities has slowed things down".

"...To reduce risk, we have taken a little longer to finalise the financial structure of the project; we have that now and the project is looking more valuable than it did initially".

"...While there has been a development delay, we have been able to lock in a reliable timeline for production and are looking at a launch in October this year".

Now, this Message Statement is acceptable. It covers the important points in less than 30 seconds. However, to make it more *vivid* - clear and memorable - we could tweak it and make it shorter. For example:

Message Statement:

"The project is behind because opportunities were found to make the new products 50% more profitable, and taking advantage of these opportunities caused a delay. However, the delays are under control: we have been able to lock in a reliable timeline for production and an October launch."

This version of the Message Statement only takes 15 seconds to say. Why don't you test it out loud yourself now. Imagine you're wrapping up your presentation, so you might start with the words:

> **"So, just to wrap up...** *The project is behind because opportunities were found to make the new products 50% more profitable, and taking advantage of these opportunities caused a delay. However, the delays are under control - we've been able to lock in a reliable timeline for production and an October launch."*

Does it contain most of the crucial information? Yes. Does it feel like an appropriate end to a professional presentation? Yes. Is it short enough to be remembered, recalled and repeated by the listeners? Probably - depending on the real situation in this imaginary organisation with these imaginary board members.

Now, you are the speaker, so *you* will decide on the precise wording for yourself. This process focuses your thinking and gives you the flexibility to reword the Message Statement. For example, a rewording might be:

> *"This project will successfully provide the range of new products we need. It is behind schedule because we identified the chance to increase profitability by a further 50%, and decided to invest the time to pursue that opportunity. We are on track for a successful launch in October this year, in time for Christmas."*

4 Message Statement tips

1. Be specific.

The 'so what?' test is great to make sure your wording is clear and specific: Imagine a person in your audience stands up and shouts, "So what?" or "Who cares?" when they hear your message. This is an excellent way to attack your message to ensure it's vivid. Stay away from vague terms and generic language if possible. If you can't think of specifics, think harder.

2. State the obvious.

A lot of people worry about offending the audience by being too 'basic'. In my experience, failing to state the basic facts is a bigger problem.

3. Don't neglect the negatives.

Consider the negatives as well as the positives. It's natural to focus solely on positives, but it's a trap. Failing to address perceived flaws ignores areas where the audience is looking to be convinced. And, looking objectively at the negatives can help you anticipate crucial questions. By integrating the answers to potential negatives, you inspire more confidence in your ideas.

4. A Message Statement is not usually a question.

Don't end with a question like: *'How could you not agree?'* or *'What more can I say!?'* or *'Why would you waste this opportunity?'*. Questions don't close the loop on your idea - they open it. And may focus the audience's mind on the reasons *not* to think or do what you suggest. Sure, there are exceptions. Branding messages like 'Got milk?' have worked well to get people thinking about drinking more milk (with a multi million dollar budget and repetition over decades), but a question implies the need for an answer. It's open to interpretation, so if you don't provide one the audience will. And it may not be the answer you want.

Recap of the Message Statement stage

Your Message Statement is drawn from the results of three questions:

1. *WHO are you talking to?*

2. *WHAT do you want them to think or do?*

3. *WHY would they think or do this?*

Combine the answers to questions 2 and 3 into a rough draft of your Message Statement. Then, polish. Out loud.

THE MAGIC OF CHUNKING

Structure underpins many great speeches. Remember Joe, the executive at Paramount Pictures in the example at the start of this book? The thing we haven't talked about yet was the lynchpin to the success of his presentation: the *'Chunk Structure'*.

When we started working on his presentation he had a deck of 80 slides (and growing) and was overwhelmed with all the content. So, we set the slides aside and created a Message Statement to guide us (which was, in a nutshell, that his team had a solid plan to promote the new Tom Cruise movie). Then I hit Joe with an ultimatum: "Everything you want to talk about has to fit under 2, 3 or 4 headings. No more. Got it?"

"Mmm, ok then", he said. Then I asked firmly,

> *"So, how many headings do you need, and what will they be called?"*

It's this simple question that drives the creation of a well-structured presentation. He chose 3 'headings' that reflected the 3 main stages of the plan - a 3 chunk structure.

Each 'chunk' can be thought of as a mini-presentation (within the main presentation) with its own beginning and end. So, the essence of the chunk structure is this: Identify a small number of themes/categories/sections; each has a **heading** which helps you decide what information goes where. It's a simple, reliable and fast way of sorting ideas and identifying takeaway points. Some of my clients call it the 'Magic Structure' because it helps pull all their ideas together so easily.

But first, let's look at why the chunking principle is so powerful.

Chunking is all round us

The human mind craves structure. Ideas and information are more memorable and easier to absorb when they are arranged using patterns or structures. There are many ways we do this, however the simple concept of chunks and chunking is the most universal. Chunking is all around us. It's one of the main ways we make sense of the world. Here are just a few examples: books have chapters, which are broken into paragraphs, which are broken into sentences. Imagine trying to read a book that was just one long paragraph.

Computers sort files and documents into folders (so do actual, physical filing cabinets). Science and biology would be impossible to teach without 'scientific classification'. For example, biological classification groups all living things into a hierarchy that includes Class, Order, Family, Genus, Species. Which is basically chunks and sub-chunks.

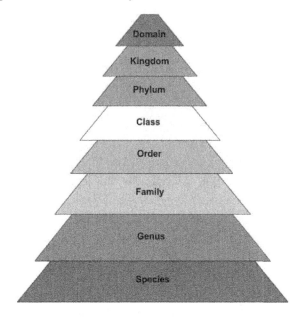

Every hierarchy is an arrangement of items (objects, names, values, categories, etc.) in which the items are represented as being 'above', 'below', or 'at the same level as' one another. The segmentation of information is found everywhere. It's all chunks, man!

Smart marketers break product offerings into chunks in the form of options. 'You have three choices: regular, large and extra-large'. We feel better about our decisions when we can focus on 2 or 3 options.

The mind loves chunks

The mind just loves chunks. They allow the mind to feel like it can manage the information, because it's defined, not open-ended. And it gives us something to look forward to, for example, 'What number are we up to in the countdown?!' When I worked in radio, we discovered through research, that countdowns were a surefire way of keeping people listening:

- The 'top 10 rock songs'
- The 'top 20 guitar songs'
- The 'top 15 love songs from the 80s'
- 'Celebrity X's top 5 songs'
- The 'top 6 rock guitar love songs from 1992', etc, etc.

In fact, we kept scouring the research to see when listeners would get sick of lists and countdowns - and they never did! This helped us to create number 1 radio stations across the country.

Books and articles that state the number of things they'll cover in the title, make their information easier to digest. *The Seven Habits of Highly Effective People* is quite a fat, detailed book, but its title and corresponding structure make it more digestible, memorable and repeatable.

Notice how tempting it is for you to read an article with the "Top 5 reasons why...". Notice *how many* of those lists we see. The reason is simple – they are hard for the human mind to resist. Examples of chunking are everywhere, simply because the human mind becomes overwhelmed without them. We need chunks! You may not be aware of it, but we all use variations on the chunking principle to make sense of the world. Have you seen this kind of example...

I cdnuolt blveiee taht I cluod aulaclty uesdnatnrd waht I was rdanieg.

The phaonmneal pweor of the hmuan mnid Aoccdrnig to rscheearch taem at Cmabrigde Uinervtisy, it deosn't mttaer in waht oredr the ltteers in a wrod are, the olny iprmoatnt tihng is taht the frist and lsat ltteer be in the rghit pclae.

The rset can be a taotl mses and you can sitll raed it wouthit a porbelm. Tihs is bcuseae the huamn mnid deos not raed ervey lteter by istlef, but the wrod as a wlohe. Such a cdonition is arppoipately cllaed Typoglycemia.

Amzanig huh? Yuo awlyas thought slpeling was ipmorantt!

Notice the 3rd to last sentence, '...the human mind does not read every letter by itself, but the word as a whole'. The start and the end of a chunk, or anything, are the clearest 'hooks' in the mind. So, put the first letter and the last letter in the right place and the mind can make sense of gibberish. In the same way, getting the start and the end of your speech right will help your audience make sense of all the boring rubbish in the middle. Well, hopefully it's not full of boring rubbish, but there is truth to the relative importance of the start and end of a speech. More tips on mastering the start and end of your speech later.

You can't recall a phone number without chunks

Write down your phone number now. You can do it on the margin right here... Read it out loud. Go on, read it out loud for real, it will help me make a point that will make you a better communicator.

Did you pause at some point while you were speaking or did every number have the same timing and inflection? We all pause at some point to allow the separation of the sections. So, why does a phone number have spaces after 3 or 4 digits? Computers don't need them. In fact, computers don't like them - the spaces, dashes, dots and parenthesis used in phone numbers can confuse database software. It's us humans who need to segment the numbers.

Now, read it out loud again, but change the place where you pause. In other words, change the chunking format. If your number is, say, 714-390-8302, read it out loud as 71-439-083-02.

How does it sound?! Has anyone ever said your phone number to you using a different chunking format? What happens to your brain when they do? It doesn't work properly! Your brain won't recognise it because it remembers the chunks, more than the individual digits. This is an important thing to understand. And a powerful tool to use when you communicate. When we don't give the mind the structure it needs our brain becomes overwhelmed and skips a beat.

So, the answer to the title question above, 'Can you recall your own phone number?' is, 'only if it's chunked the way I like it!' This gives you a hint at the leverage of chunking when you communicate. If you don't structure your information well, there's less chance your audience will recall it.

'I chunk, therefore I can think'

Philosopher Rene Descartes distilled the essence of his philosophical enquiries into the statement,

'I think, therefore I am'.

For practical purposes, he might have said,

'I chunk, therefore I can think'.

My first exposure to chunking was in Tom Peters' book *In Search Of Excellence* in the mid 1980s. I met him once and thanked him for the chunking idea that I 'stole' from him. He smiled and said, "You're welcome, I stole it from someone else of course."

I found that the study of the 'chunking' principle began with a research paper published by George A. Miller at Harvard University back in 1956. In his paper, *The magical number seven, plus or minus two: Some limits on our capacity for processing information*, Miller showed that the human mind needs to use 'a process of organising or grouping the input into familiar units or chunks'.

He found the maximum number of things the human mind could

remember or work with was between 5 and 9. However, to recall more than 5 things requires a structure or memory device of some kind.

There is more recent research that demonstrates that 5 things is the upper limit - but you don't need the research to know it. Ask yourself: 'How many things can I remember without writing them down or using a memory device?' What's your answer? For most people its 4 or 5.

Can you remember all the names of the 7 dwarfs? Most people can't do this on the spot, because 7 things is too many things to recall without a structure. I've asked the 7-dwarf-question to thousands of people at seminars and conferences - and even those who confidently put up their hands, begin to stumble around 5 dwarf names. However, there is usually no problem remembering the names of the 3 stooges.

What's the best design for a phone number?

Let's go back to phone numbers. Interestingly, Miller's research was used to *design* the current U.S. phone number. That's right, in the 1960s a group of people sat around a table and *designed* the best format for a phone number, for the Bell Telephone Company.

The situation was this: there was a massive increase in the number of phones in use and a major upgrade of the telephone exchanges was taking place. There was a need for a format that would allow hundreds of millions of numbers, but still be easy to remember. Bell Telephone knew that if people couldn't easily remember phone numbers, 2 things would happen: 1) they were likely to make fewer calls - resulting in less revenue and 2) there would be more wrong numbers and greater frustration.

The format they came up with has been a great success. 7 digits, broken into 2 chunks, e.g. 123 4567.

A total of 7, broken in to 2 chunks of less than 5.

And the fact that the first and second chunks are *different* - the first chunk has 3 numbers and the second chunk has 4 - also makes them easier to remember.

You might be thinking, 'Hang on Cam, there are actually more than 7 digits in a phone number'. Yes, that's true, e.g. (456) 123 4567. But can you also see that placing extra digits in (parentheses), signifies to the mind they are clearly a separate chunk, making the longer number easier to process, remember and recall.

It's amazing how our ability to recall information is boosted when it is chunked. We can recall 10 or 15 numbers in a Chunk Structure - compared to 3 or 4 numbers without a Chunk Structure.

A 300% increase!

My brother lives in London so I need to dial 16 or 17 digits to call him (depending on which country I call from). However, I can remember all these digits because I know the chunking format:

- [3 digits to get out of the country]
- [2 digits to get into England]
- [4 digit area code]
- [7 digit number in 2 chunks] Easy!

Oh, it's a different category? I'm happy to pay more!

Organisations chunk their products and services to have more options to raise prices. And we buy it! For example; 30 years ago there were 2 possible fees for a phone call. A fixed fee for the call and a fee per minute. Now we have the wonders of: connection fees, account-keeping fees, monthly line rental, fee-per-minute and flagfall (the person who thought of 'flagfall' should go down in history as a sage. This was the idea of a new fee for the receiver answering your call, while at the same time the fee-per-minute begins. Genius!).

Telecommunications companies discovered that this appeared more reasonable than continuously raising the fee per minute. We accept the fees because these are separate 'things' in our mind - as opposed to the fee per minute continuing to increase.

Chunking to sell an idea

Here's a story about a charming old guy called 'Farmer Jim'. It shows how a chunked conversation can engage a listener, create curiosity about the next point, increase the attention span of a listener and help them recall the key points.

Farmer Jim was at an agricultural show when he stopped at a display of shiny, red, new tractors. Jim wasn't in the market for a tractor, but he stopped to gather information. The Tractor Guy asked Jim which tractor he was currently operating.

"A ten-year-old John Deere," Jim replied. "It does the job, so I don't need a new one - and I can't really afford to replace it."

"Fair enough. Replacing a tractor is one of your biggest expenses. I find there are 3 *things* that come into play when farmers are considering a changeover." Tractor guy expanded on those 3 things:

- The **limitations** of older tractors, particularly reliability and cost of operation.

- The **new technology** that makes tractors incredibly efficient and amazingly comfortable – "It's like sitting in a car" – reducing fatigue.

- The **return on investment**. "Your monthly outlay won't be a lot more than you're paying now, and will be more than paid back by the output you'll get from the machine."

The two kept talking, with Jim asking questions, testing claims and seeking more detail. But *the entire conversation was now structured around the 3 chunks outlined at the start* - making it much easier to process the information, think clearly and get satisfying answers. Jim even felt like *he* was driving the conversation as he pushed for explanations on the 3 issues.

That night, Jim spoke to his wife and business partner, "I think it's time to upgrade the tractor".

"Why?" she said. "You've always said the one we have gets the job done just fine?"

"True, but there are 3 reasons it now makes sense." Jim outlined 1) the **limitations** of his current tractor and 2) the benefits of the **new technology**. When his wife raises the question of cost, 3) Jim has the answer, the financing and **return on investment**.

Very quickly, both were comfortable with the decision to buy a new bright red tractor.

It's important to realise that the Chunk Structure is not sneaky or manipulative. It's simply clearer and easier to process information when it is chunked effectively. It's the way our minds prefer to work. The tragedy is that good ideas fail to take hold because they are communicated in a way that's unstructured and hard to follow. These wasted opportunities happen too often.

There's something magical in this example. Not only was Tractor Guy able to deliver a clear and understandable message to Jim, but the message he delivered was *transferable*. Jim was able to go home and convey the same message, with almost all the detail, to his wife.

Tractor Guy knew exactly what he was doing.

Chunking ideas engages people early

First, he engaged Jim early by mentioning that there were *3 things* farmers usually consider when buying a new tractor. By flagging 3 things – 3 chunks – right up front, we are *pulled* into the conversation. We need to know what the 3 things are and we listen more intently as they are delivered.

This is a huge benefit to the audience: chunks create interest – suspense – by placing an expectation in the listeners' minds. Once Jim registered that there were '3 things', he decided to stay long enough to hear all three.

The second thing Tractor Guy did with the Chunk Structure was bring Jim into the discussion - and help him feel he was in control of the information. How? The chunked structure gave Jim a framework to explore this idea. His *own* framework. And this helped make it a *transferable* idea. The framework made it easier for Jim to *recall information* to sell the idea to his decision-making partner.

The same method will work in your presentations. Breaking your ideas into chunks makes it easier for your audience to take that message and share it with others. So, chunks make it easier to create our holy grail: a simple, clear, transferable message.

There's a third reason why chunks are good for your audience: they *reduce the amount of thinking* the audience needs to do. Listener overwhelm is the biggest challenge for a communicator. By providing a ready-made structure, the listener's mind can relax as you gently add the details. And they feel more comfortable listening to you.

However, when a speaker has no clear structure, the audience is forced to create their own. There are 2 disadvantages to this: 1) the structure they create may not be the one you had in mind, so they recall different information than you had intended, and 2) IKEA syndrome - the extra mental energy required to 'build their own structure' increases mental fatigue. And attention spans are constantly reducing. People are not really conscious of why their attention keeps drifting, they just find you less interesting as a speaker!

Chunking can make you seem wise and thoughtful

So, generally speaking, communication that is chunked will be: more interesting, easier to recall and share with others, make the speaker seem more organised, easier to follow, make the speaker seem wiser and better prepared and, as a result, make the audience feel more connected and *like* the speaker more.

It's also true that communication *without* a clear structure is less interesting; harder to follow; harder to recall and share with others; makes the speaker seem disorganised; makes the speaker seem less informed and amateurish; and, as a result, makes us have less confidence in what the speaker says. That's how powerful the effect of chunking can be on your presentations.

In a nutshell, chunking makes it easier for you to *prepare* and *deliver* a presentation, and easier for your audience to *absorb* and *recall* your information.

So, let's look at how to build your next presentation using the chunk structure...

STRUCTURING YOUR IDEAS, STEP-BY-STEP

There are 2 ways to lay out your Chunk Structure:

1. Column format (with sticky notes)
2. Text format

    See below for both options.

1. Column format

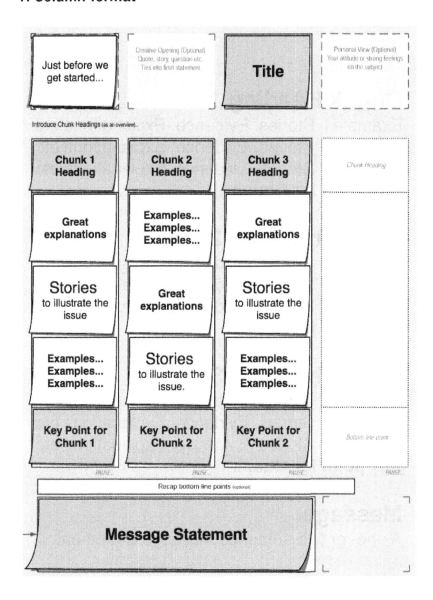

2. Text format

Title

Chunk Heading 1

Examples. Stories. Evidence. Explanations etc.
Examples. Stories. Evidence. Explanations etc.
Examples. Stories. Evidence. Explanations etc.
Key point for Chunk

Chunk Heading 2

Examples. Stories. Evidence. Explanations etc.
Examples. Stories. Evidence. Explanations etc.
Examples. Stories. Evidence. Explanations etc.
Key point for Chunk

Chunk heading 3

Examples. Stories. Evidence. Explanations etc.
Examples. Stories. Evidence. Explanations etc.
Examples. Stories. Evidence. Explanations etc.
Key point for Chunk

Message

A one- or two-sentence Message Statement...

Notice that the *column* format and the *text* format are essentially the same. Some people prefer the *text* format while others prefer the *column* format. Use the one that feels better for you.

Chunk Structure step-by-step

Let's build a Chunk Structure step-by-step. This is often done with Sticky Notes, but you could do it on the back of a napkin once you're familiar with the format.

Start with Message Statement and Title

You've already completed your Message Statement, simply add it to the bottom of the Chunk Structure.

Next, your title. A title is an opportunity that most people don't take advantage of. A great test for a good title is to imagine an attendee at a conference with you and 9 other speakers. They only have time to attend 2 speeches, and must choose them based solely on their title. Does yours illuminate the issue and entice them to attend?

A good title can also work as a *window* to the interesting parts of your presentation. For example:

'How we'll meet our sales targets' is better than 'March update'.

'How the new system will save you time', is better than 'The new system'.

'Today I'm going to tell you 3 stories from my life' (Steve Jobs' Stanford speech) is better than 'My life'.

Define your chunk headings

Now we need to give each chunk a heading. Your Message Statement is your guide here. Clarifying your chunk headings can be as simple as:

Read your Message Statement out loud to focus your attention.

Pause.

Now think about ALL the things you want to cover in your talk. Then decide on 2, 3 or 4 chunk headings. Everything you want to cover needs to fit under one of these headings. Get them down on paper quickly - you can always change them later. No matter how complex your presentation, they can be simple, high level headings, like:

1. The opportunity.
2. The market profile.
3. The return on investment.
4. How we can work together.

One example that can apply to many subjects is a timeline:

1. The history of the issue ...
2. The current situation ...
3. What might happen in the future ...
4. Next steps

Another example that can be used in a broad range of situations is:

1. The problem.
2. The options.
3. The solution.

Now, test your headings out loud - as though you were starting your talk and giving an overview. For example:

> *"Hi, this presentation is about Project X. And we'll look at 3 areas... Firstly, the problem we have, secondly, the options we face, and finally, the recommended solution."*

If you like the way it sounds when you test it out loud, continue to the next step in your Chunk Structure. If it didn't sound clear or complete, tweak it until you're happy.

Tweaking the wording of your chunk headings

Keep the wording of your chunk headings simple, but make sure the language is relevant and interesting to your audience. For example: A Human Resources Manager from the head office of a franchise chain was making a speech to retail store managers about succession planning. She had created a presentation structure with three chunk headings:

1. Succession planning
2. Performance management
3. Our company's experience.

After testing it out loud she realised that many of the store managers wouldn't be clear on what she meant by 'succession planning' or 'performance management'. These were terms they used in the HR Department, not the retail stores.

So she tweaked the chunk headings to use language that would hook her audience straight away. The reworked chunk headings were simpler and more meaningful to her listeners. (They also made it easier for her to sort her ideas.) It became:

1. What is a succession plan?
2. What exactly do you need to do to create one?
3. The benefits to you and your store.

Chunk headings give you the opportunity to grab the interest of the audience in the first 30 seconds. The right wording opens a 'container' in their mind for each chunk, making them curious to hear what falls under each heading.

Remember, it's more effective to get ideas out of your head and write something down in rough form - and then tweak. You don't need to wait until it's *all* clear in your mind before you put pen to paper. The steps of this structure will actually do some of the sorting *for you*!

Find the key point for each chunk

With your chunk headings identified, it's easy to sort your content under these headings. However, it's a good idea to find the **end point** for each chunk first. This stops you getting bogged down in details. My radio announcer friends used to say "The best way to write a 'talk break' is to start at the end. The secret is to know how you are going to wrap up. Then the rest is easy to fill..."

The same goes for the sections of your talk. Find the key point for each chunk. The key point is a mini-message or 'bottom-line point' of the ideas you've explained in the chunk. The best way to *find* your bottom-line point for a chunk is to read this sentence out loud:

"So, in relation to [state the chunk heading], the point is..."

This drives your brain to crystallise your main point effortlessly. It's many times more effective to do this out loud, than to just write what comes to mind. Almost magically, your mind will respond with words that flow and make sense. Here are 2 examples:

So, in relation to [the problem], the point is... [the current product has a 30% failure rate].

So, what is [a succession plan?], it's... [a plan you need to have to ensure your business thrives].

With bottom-line points defined, 'filling' chunks with details is much easier. You see at a glance how the chunk ends, making it easy to see if you need more information, better examples or supporting data - or whether you can cut information because you already have enough to make your point. It's much faster to review and edit at the *outline stage*, because you're just tweaking key points, not wrestling with the full presentation.

Fill the chunks with examples, stories, evidence

Now that you have prioritised your key points you can add detail without agonising over it.

Include evidence, stories, examples, research, statistics or images or video (if using slides). It's good to use a mixture of these for variety, but the main thing is that each point supports your final *bottom-line point* for that chunk. Remember, people will forget most of what they hear, so our job is to use evidence, examples, etc., to support or illuminate a simple takeaway point.

It's usually best to avoid writing out full sentences at this stage. Sure, some people like to write out all the detail in 'long hand' while others will jot down just a couple of points. Do whatever works for you. But for most people, it's more effective to use bullet points. Build your case point-by-point. Use them to explain, reinforce and prove the bottom-line point you are making.

Twice the impact using half the effort

This planning process works with any subject and for presentations of any length. It makes your preparation twice as effective, using half the effort. Here are 4 benefits of the speech outline planning process.

First, it reduces procrastination. You focus on one section at a time, produce a 'first draft' quickly and then go back and refine. Most people struggle too long to feel 'clear' before getting their first draft done.

Second, it helps you identify persuasive arguments. When you see your ideas laid out in a chunk structure, it's easier to identify patterns and connections within your information. This helps you discover compelling points more naturally. The creative process flows with less friction.

Third, it helps you stay on track. Chunking makes it easier to go away and come back to your work without losing your way. You refine by simply changing headings or adding or subtracting sub-points.

Fourth, it saves time. The chunk structure is a massive short-cut compared to writing out a full speech, then reviewing that full speech 3 or 4 times to refine your ideas. It stops the mental 'train wreck' where all the ideas, questions and information surrounding your talk, pile up and block clear thinking. This makes the planning process feel effortless.

STRUCTURE HELPS YOU <u>DELIVER</u> A SPEECH MORE POWERFULLY

Remember, the START and END of a chunk are used as hooks by the mind. In fact, the start and the end of anything is compelling to your listeners. So use signpost words for emphasis. Words like '*firstly*', '*secondly*' and so on. And phrases like '*Now let's move on to...*', are effective for marking the beginning of a new point. When your audience's attention wanders, these words pull them back. The same goes for ending a section: use language like, '*So the main thing to remember about XYZ is...*' to wrap up an idea.

5 ways Chunk Structure helps you deliver a talk

Here are 5 ways the Chunk Structure helps you deliver a talk with greater impact and reduced effort.

First, the Chunk Structure makes it easier to **remember** what you want to say. And knowing your chunk headings and key points makes it much easier to recall the details within each section.

Second, it shows you what to **emphasise**. Many presentations have the same emphasis all the way through, like a song without a chorus, and they miss the opportunity to hit the high notes of the presentation. The Chunk Structure provides natural points of emphasis – the start and end of each chunk. Which is where you placed your most important takeaway messages. Nice.

Third, it controls **rambling**. People ramble when they're not sure of their *end point*. As they wonder if the audience is getting 'it', they add more words. This uncertain tone sounds meek - and weakens their ability to persuade. It's like they're flying a plane and don't know where to land. Of course the passengers feel uncomfortable! Conversely, emphasising points with certainty makes the speaker seem credible and convincing.

Fourth, the Chunk Structure gives you **flexibility**. You can easily reduce or expand the length of your talk without changing the structure. Imagine this: you've been given 30 minutes for your talk, but other speakers go over time and you're asked to fit your talk into 15 minutes. What happens?

> *Scenario 1: You've rehearsed your speech word-for-word. Now, you've been asked to cut it in half. But you don't know what to cut. Flustered, you race through your speech trying to squeeze it all in, apologising often.*

> *Scenario 2: Your talk is structured into three or four chunks, and each of those has stories, examples and so on, that lead to a takeaway point. You simply leave out a few details in each chunk and end on your takeaway point as planned. The audience hears all the important stuff and has no idea what you cut. You're able to speak calmly and end with your vivid message, just as planned. Sweet.*

Fifth, the Chunk Structure helps you speak with more **confidence**. When your talk is easier to remember, and has the flexibility to adjust to real-world situations, you feel in control. It's manageable. You're ready, and you know it. You speak more naturally and with greater certainty.

Steve Jobs uses Chunk Structure in 'Stanford commencement speech'

Now you know how to Chunk a speech, watch Steve Jobs deliver one. Perhaps Jobs' most famous speech, this was made to students of Stanford University in June 2005. Go to https://www.youtube.com/watch?v=UF8uR6Z6KLc.

This speech holds the record as the most viewed. The top 5 TED talks have between 20 and 30 million views, while this speech has around 35 million. It's 15 minutes long, and tells engaging stories and shares unique life lessons. It's an interesting, engaging and inspirational speech. The reason I mention it now is that it's built and delivered on the 3-chunk structure we have been teaching since 1999.

There are no slides, none of the typical, beautiful visuals to support his words. It's not perfectly rehearsed (Jobs stands at a lectern and reads the speech). In other words, it has few of the qualities that traditional experts highlight as the secret to Steve Jobs' communication brilliance.

When communication experts write about Steve Jobs, they often lose focus on the core of all his talks. His core is always *message, structure* and *natural style*. This gets lost in the 10 tips that include 'prepare and practice excessively', 'avoid reading from notes', 'express your passion' (where does passion come from - clarity), 'sell dreams not products', 'introduce a villain', etc. Sure, these techniques can add impact, however, we improve fastest when we prioritise.

Think of the 10 or 15 tips as cream on the cake. Cream is wonderful and most of the tips are helpful. I'm just suggesting you make sure the solid foundations are mastered *before* getting distracted by tasty sprinkles.

You see, Steve Jobs' most famous speech is built on 3 simple things *you* can master. Message and structure to give clarity to the ideas, and natural style to add life to your words.

Now, I didn't coach Steve Jobs, nor am I suggesting he was reading my material (although it's possible - I wrote to him about a marketing issue in the late 1990s), but this speech is a wonderful example of the Vivid Method in action!

Here's how it looks in the Chunk Structure.

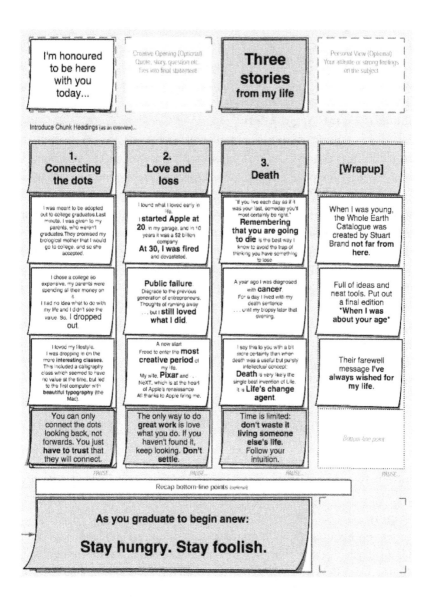

Here is the basic structure of Jobs' speech. (By the way, this is a summary of what he said, not a full transcript. The full transcript can be found online if you want to check out the details.)

Scene setting

"I'm honored to be here with you today. I never graduated. This is the closest I've been to a college graduation."

Title

*"Today, I want to tell you **three stories** from my life."*

Chunk 1. Connecting the dots

Tells a story about dropping out of college but staying as a 'drop in'. He could attend any class that interested him, not those he needed to graduate. This included a calligraphy class which seemed to have no value, but led to the first computer with beautiful typography (the Mac)."

Bottom line point: *"You can only connect the dots looking back, not forwards. You just have to trust that they will connect."*

Chunk 2. Love and loss

Tells the story of being fired by Apple. An embarrassing failure. Then spent the next 10 years working hard with no public success. But it turned out to be the most creative period of his life: he met his wife, started Pixar and NeXT - which Apple purchased and brought him back as CEO.

Bottom line point: *"The only way to do great work is love what you do. If you haven't found it, keep looking. Don't settle."*

Chunk 3. Death

Talks about death and his own battles with cancer, but adds that remembering you're going to die is the best way I know to avoid the trap of thinking you have something to lose. Death is Life's change agent reminding you to follow your own path.

Bottom line point: *"Time is limited; don't waste it living someone else's life. Follow your intuition."*

Wrap-up

He sets up his message with another story about a publication called the Whole Earth Catalog. He uses repetition and language to connect with his listeners: *"it was created not far from here... They put out a final edition when I was your age. Their farewell message was 'Stay hungry. Stay foolish'. I've always wished that for myself."*

Message

"As you graduate to begin anew, I wish that for you: Stay hungry. Stay foolish."

Kutcher channels Jobs, gets quoted chunk-for-chunk

As a short aside, it was interesting to see how Ashton Kutcher's 2013 Teen Choice speech was covered in the media. Ashton Kutcher played Steve Jobs in the biographical film called simply, 'Jobs'.

See below how this Aug '13 Business Insider News article transferred Kutcher's 3 key points exactly as Kutcher wanted them to be shared. In fact, it's got a clearer structure than most articles, simply by copying the structure of the speech. A clear structure helps make your ideas transferable - and get shared.

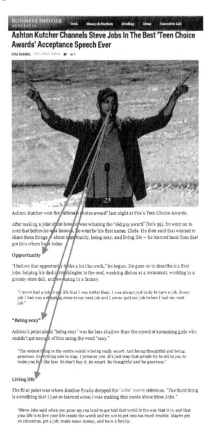

HOW TO REHEARSE IN HALF THE TIME

Let's look at how to practice and rehearse your talk...

Wasted effort: practice does not make perfect

When my son was 2 years old he loved to 'drive' his toy car, especially after spending time in a real car. We would arrive home and the first thing he would do was jump in that toy car and turn the steering wheel hard back and forth in an attempt to get his car moving.

Unaware that there are foot pedals to control forward motion, he worked on the erroneous assumption that turning the steering wheel propels a car forward. All he saw was 1) his dad turning the steering wheel and 2) the car moving. The more he saw these 2 things happen together, the more he thought they were linked – and the harder he tried to turn the wheel on his little car to make it move. It never worked.

The frustration I witnessed in my son is similar to the frustration I've seen in people trying to propel their public speaking skills forward based on the wrong premise. You may have heard it's all about practice, practice, PRACTICE. But that's not the whole story. Like my son in his car, people often approach practice with an erroneous assumption: that long rehearsals and frequent practice will automatically make them better. This is only partly true.

Of course, there are many benefits to rehearsing; you can hear how your talk sounds out loud, test the flow, and reduce uncertainty by becoming more familiar with the ideas. However, it's the *way* you practice that makes all the difference.

Without knowing what to focus on, many people see practice as a painful chore that will only end with an anxiety-ridden presentation. It saddens me to see people approach rehearsal with the look of a beaten boxer about to face another round of being thumped in the head.

If you focus on memorising a speech word-for-word or hope that slick design will fully engage your audience, you may get discouraged when you're still nervous or ineffective.

With a clear understanding of what really drives (no pun intended) confidence and clarity-of-mind during a presentation, you can use a shortcut that allows you to practice for a fraction of the time and yet feel twice as certain. Practice doesn't need to be difficult, and it doesn't need to be time consuming.

Of course, you should do whatever works for you. If you get better results from rehearsing 20 times, then go for it. However, if you'd like a short cut, try this...

The 1-minute rehearsal!

I've used the word 'magic' a couple of times in this book. That's because many of our clients have used it over the years. Is it valid? Well, some of these techniques do seem to magically dissolve blocks, or provide an effortless way forward that previously involved a lot of time and frustration. The 1-minute rehearsal can have this magical impact. You don't need to learn every word of your speech. You just need to get clear and practice the key points in your structure. In other words:

1. The start.

2. The chunk headings and bottom-line points.

3. The wrap-up including your Message Statement.

This will only take you a minute or so, no matter how long the speech. So, grab your 1-page chunk structure and read it out loud - skipping the details. As you move through the structure, simply pause or say 'Blah Blah Blah' in place of the details *within* each chunk.

Example of a 1-minute rehearsal

"Hi, this presentation is about [your title...].
In exploring this idea, we'll cover 3 areas, firstly, [chunk 1 heading],

secondly [chunk 2 heading] and finally [chunk 3 heading].
So, let's have a look at [chunk 1 heading]. Blah blah... Blah blah... The key thing here is [bottom line point for chunk 1].
[pause]
Now let's look at [chunk 2 heading]. Blah blah... Blah blah... The thing to remember is [bottom line point for chunk 2].
[pause]
Finally, [chunk 3 heading]. Blah blah... Blah blah... The key point is [bottom line point for chunk 3].
[pause]
So, just to wrap up, [message statement]."

Feel free to play with the wording to suit your material and personal preferences. But you probably won't need to change the format because it suits any talk that has a structure. The basic rhythm of the 1 minute rehearsal will keep you focused on the areas you want your audience to retain and recall.

Steve Jobs Stanford speech is 2,260 words. Rehearsing at normal speed requires 15 minutes of focus and mental energy. That doesn't sound too onerous, does it? But consider that you're using a rehearsal to test and tweak your speech, so you'll stop many times and be constantly distracted from your focus on structure and key points. Now it becomes much easier to get lost in the details as your rehearsal gets close to an hour.

However, a 1-minute rehearsal allows you to test and refine your structure and key points with a fraction of the effort. And it's much more effective because you don't have to hold so much information in your mind at one time (remember the neuroscience showing that there is a tight limit to the number of things that can be held in the mind and manipulated at any one time). Here's how Steve Jobs Stanford speech would work as a 1-minute rehearsal:

Example of Steve Jobs' 1-minute rehearsal

[The Start]:
"I'm honoured to be here with you today as this is the closest I've been to a college graduation. I never graduated."
*"Today, I want to tell you **three stories from my life**. They are about 1)*

Connecting the dots in life, 2) Love and loss, and 3) Death."
[Pause]
*"So, firstly, [**Connecting the dots**]:*
Blah blah... Blah blah...
The key thing here is... that you can only connect the dots looking back, not forwards. You just have to trust they will connect. Trust your instincts."
[Pause]
*"Secondly, [**Love and loss**]:*
Blah blah... Blah blah...
The point here is... the only way to do great work is love what you do. If you haven't found it, keep looking. Don't settle."
[Pause]
*"The third thing I want to talk about is [**Death**]:*
Blah blah... Blah blah...
So remember... your time is limited; don't waste it living someone else's life. Follow your intuition."
[Wrap up including your Message Statement]
*"So just to wrap up, when I was young, there was an amazing publication called the Whole Earth Catalog, full of ideas and neat tools. On their final edition, they had the farewell message 'Stay hungry. Stay foolish'. I've always wished that for myself. As you graduate to begin anew, I wish that for you: [**Stay hungry. Stay foolish.**]"*

If Steve Jobs was sitting at his kitchen table writing this speech (which is what he did, according to the 2013 biography by Walter Isaacson), taking a minute to stand up and do a 1-minute rehearsal would give him a clear indication of the structure and flow - and whether it's conveying the key ideas he wanted it to convey. Or he could call in his wife; *'Hey honey, have you got a minute? Have a listen to this outline and tell me if you think it flows well...'*

When the structure is clear, refine the details

Once you're happy with the 1-minute version (that contains the exact words for the key points you want your audience to retain and recall), it's orders-of-magnitude easier to refine the details and finish the speech.

And you polish your speech with a feeling of clarity that makes the whole process seem fluid and effortless.

The 1-minute rehearsal is just as flexible as the chunk structure itself. You can include an overview of your chunk headings after your title, or not. You can do a long wrap-up that leads to your message, or not. Or you can do a **2-minute** or **5-minute version** if you want to test some of your explanations or bullet-point your way through your content.

You can even do a **30 second version** to help you remember the key points just before you go on stage. One of my coaching clients likes to call me within a one hour window before she makes a big speech. We only chat for a few minutes as we review her focus for the speech and go through her 1-minute rehearsal a couple of times. Practicing your 1-minute version out loud a few times can fill you with confidence.

You guessed it - say it out loud

I know I'm ranting about testing things out loud. It's just so powerful. Here's an example of the difference between rehearsing in your head, and reading your notes out loud. A few years ago, a successful professional speaker asked me to help her with her new speech. She felt the new material wasn't working on stage as well as she wanted.

At first I wasn't sure how to help. Her concepts made sense. She had a commanding presence and years of experience on the professional circuit. I asked a few questions to see if I could find a pivotal issue. One question was about rehearsal, 'How do you rehearse? Do you stand in front of a mirror or a chair or do you explain in front of your friends?'

She said, "Oh no, I rehearse in my head."

"Ah ha! There's the problem," I said.

By rehearsing in her head, she wasn't practicing words that would actually be spoken. She knew what she *meant* during rehearsal but not what she was going to *say*. It was this disconnect that was throwing her. On stage her explanations didn't feel right. They weren't as good as they seemed during rehearsal. The change to rehearsing the key points *out loud* made all the difference. She has since gone from strength to strength including making many television appearances.

VIVID METHOD PART THREE: GIVE GREAT EXPLANATIONS

EFFORTLESS DELIVERY SKILLS

Great delivery skills flow from the clarity you have about your ideas.

When you have messages and examples that bring your ideas to life, *you also* come to life. When you have genuine belief about what you are explaining, and you're comfortable in your own skin, you become effortlessly compelling.

Feeling prepared is the foundation for your improvement. And you now know how to feel prepared for your next speech or presentation. You know how to start, how to end, and you have a structure to guide you through the rest.

You know you can be *yourself.* You know that you'll be more effective and people will accept you more fully when you speak in a way that makes *you* feel most comfortable. So, a lot of your uncertainty around public speaking should be dissolved (except maybe the little bit that makes life interesting).

Therefore, this last section is about **options**.

We've been using the cake analogy, so this section is all about the icing, the cream, the cherries, the sprinkles that sit on top of your rich foundation. Or maybe even the delicious creamy custard that's stuffed in the middle of the cake.

Great explanations automatically

After a few years of teaching this 3-part method, we noticed something interesting: when people master parts 1 and 2, they start to give great explanations *automatically*. Why? Because they've discarded the distracting ideas and contradictory advice that diffuse their energy, and they're free to get on with just *explaining their stuff*, effortlessly.

In fact, if you're tired of reading, need to check your emails or feel like going for a walk along the beach, you can stop here.

Put the book down.

You already know enough to be in the top 20% of presenters.

Public speaking doesn't need to be complicated.

However, there are plenty of cool options to engage your listeners more deeply, so we might as well have a look at them.

The best way to boost your stage presence is to use techniques that **paint a clearer picture**. Accordingly, the following techniques focus on ways to amplify your ideas and add flesh to the bones of your information. They don't require acting skills, but they do offer potent ways to capture and keep your audience's attention. Try the techniques you feel will fit with your subject matter and style.

Remember, nothing is compulsory. There are no rules, just guidelines. So if you see a technique here that doesn't feel like you, ignore it. However, if you like 1 or 2 of the techniques in this section, and feel they will mesh with your style... try 'em!

HOW TO START A SPEECH

Both the start and end of a talk are important foundations, so it's worth getting good at these 'bookends'.

The most reliable way to start is to state your title and give an **overview** of your chunks. For example:

> "G'day. This talk is about [title], and we'll cover [chunk 1 heading], [chunk 2 heading] and then [chunk 3 heading]. OK, let's look at [chunk 1 heading]..."

...And you're into the guts of your talk with no waffle.

The 'overview' satisfies your listeners' questions

As simple as this sounds, it's a powerful way to start. It includes an overview which satisfies 2 questions in the mind of your audience: 1) *'where is this talk going?'* and 2) *'is it relevant to me?'*. The overview sets the scene and helps the audience feel comfortable and curious about your content.

Think about a typical person in your audience. Their mind is full of to-do lists and daydreams, and you walk on stage. They've sat through boring presentations in the past and wonder if yours will be interesting. They look at you... pondering how much attention to give.

The overview ensures you start with clarity and certainty.

We know that all anxiety is caused by uncertainty, but we haven't yet focused that idea on the audience. When your listeners are uncertain about where your presentation is going, or whether you'll be covering things of interest to them, they feel a little uncomfortable - uncertain. Yet when you make it clear where you're headed, and they can see your talk will be relevant, they feel strangely satisfied. When you put them into this comfortable state at the start of a speech, it activates their minds and makes them feel better about you as a speaker.

An optional introduction

The overview is simple and reliable, but short. An introduction is one way to add 'flavour' to your presentation. It can include any creative idea, such as those listed later in this section. For example, a story, quote, metaphor, top and tail, provocative question, etc.

You may have noticed that the top row of the Chunk Structure diagram includes 3 grey boxes. They are: 1) Scene setting, 2) Creative opening & closing and 3) Personal view.

1. Scene setting

The scene setting part of your introduction can be used to cover things like: the situation that led to this talk, your role, your company's credentials or 'housekeeping issues' like where the coffee is, when you'll break, if there is a handout, etc.

This is also the time for the awesome "**Just before we get started...**" tactic covered in the first pages of this book. This technique can transform a cold or hostile environment into a relaxed and welcoming one. When you walk out as the speaker, the silence in the room, and all the eyes focused on you, can seem empty, cheerless and a little daunting. If you don't do anything to address this energy void, it may take a long time for the room to warm up on its own.

A lot of speakers mistake this common, understandable starting energy as a difficult audience. They walk out and think, 'Oh god...this is a tough room!' But, if you take on what you perceive as 'the negative mood of the room', you set it in stone. You might think, 'They're all serious here, so I'll be serious too'. And you just hope somehow it will change.

But why would it?

As soon as the audience sees that you're serious, uncomfortable or formal, they think 'Ok, that's the style of this talk' and follow it as well. It becomes a self-reinforcing loop between speaker and audience.

But you don't have to fall into this trap. Think of it this way: there is no existing 'mood of the room', because they are all waiting for you to define it!

The beautiful thing is that you, as the speaker, have much more power and control to reset the mood of the room than you realise. So, even if it's a cold room, you walk in and say very casually... 'Just before we get started...' And everybody relaxes. The pressure of the start dissolves, and we are in conversation mode. Here are some examples:

> *Just before we get started, I want to ask you a question, tell me... (and then ask them a question)*

Or...

> *Just before we get started, let me give you some background on why we're all together in this room today... (and then give them the background)*

Or...

> *Just before we get started, we're talking about a project update today, but let's look at why this project is happening in the first place... (and then explain).*

You can use this technique to ease into a presentation, get your pace right, ensure your breathing is comfortable and adjust to the room.

2. Creative Opening (top and tail)

You can use an introduction to pique interest or paint a picture with a story, chart, dramatic statement or provocative question. For example:

> *"We will never run out of oil."*

> *"Half of what you know about health is wrong."*

> *"Imagine living 100 years ago..."*

You can be as dramatic as you feel is appropriate, but make sure your creativity is **linked to the message** you want them to remember. There's no point in having them remember your inventive opening, then forget your message. The best way to link your creative opening with your message is to think in terms of a 'top and tail'.

A 'top and tail' means starting your speech (**the top**) with a statement or idea, and then ending the speech with the same statement or idea (**the tail**) by linking it to your final message.

For example, start by holding up a document titled 'Peak Oil', (which states that the world is running out of oil) and say 'Today I'll explain why we will *never* run out of oil'. Then go through your presentation showing the new oil discoveries. At the end you hold the document up again as you state your message that we'll never run out of oil, supported by your key points. (You could even rip the document up at the end if you like the drama of it).

Your 'top and tail' might simply start with a quote that relates to your message. At the end, you recall that quote and link it to your message.

3. Personal view

If you have a strong opinion about the topic, or think it's especially important, tell them so at the start. Sharing your emotions can have great impact. A personal view might include your reason for speaking, your excitement or your disappointment. For example:

> *"Before we get into the details, I'd like to recognise how hard the team has worked on this proposal. I'm **really proud** and excited with what we've come up with. So let's have a look at it..."*

Or...

> *"Today we are reviewing the quarterly sales figures and I think we have a **problem!** The numbers are really disappointing. It breaks my heart after all the hard work we've put in. [Pause] Ok, this presentation is about a smarter way to increase sales."*

So, the introduction can include the options listed above, or others that you cherry-pick from the next section. Use your own judgement, however a shorter introduction is usually better than a long one.

HOW TO END A SPEECH

The universe has no end.

Doesn't that blow your mind a little? When you look up in the sky, it doesn't end. Ever. Han Solo and Chewbacca could travel at light speed in the Millennium Falcon *forever*, and they'd never get to the 'far reaches of the galaxy', because it just keeps going on and on. (Which is what some presentations feel like.)

This is difficult for humans to fathom. Our brain can't process things that don't end. Yet this creates an opportunity to satisfy people's craving for completion. With a tidy ending, your audience will process everything you've said with less effort, *and* find it easier to remember.

Last words linger. Don't waste them

The end of your talk is automatically a focal point for your listeners. The point in time where you say your last words, is the most favourable time to embed a message. However, it's amazing how many presenters seem surprised by the ending of their own talk! Have you noticed this? The final slide comes up and the speaker says,

> *"Oh, um, I guess that's it. So… any questions?"*

This is your big ending?! Certainly not the way to gain credibility and clarity at the end of your talk. The end of your presentation is your golden moment to leverage all the words you've said up to that point.

A weak ending diminishes your credibility. Why? When the audience doesn't get the structure they crave, your ideas seem a little weaker, less important, less memorable, less *complete*. And because you're the speaker who delivered this unsatisfying combination, you don't appear to have as much authority. There are a few options in the way you end, so it's helpful

to think of the end as having 2 stages:
 1) Your wrap-up.
 2) Your final message.

Your wrap-up

A wrap-up can include a *recap* of your main points. This might be as simple as repeating 'bottom line points' from the end of each chunk. It's not required, but might flow well leading up to your message, especially for long talks. Test it out loud to find out.

Your wrap-up can also be a *setup* for your big ending, like Steve Jobs' Stanford Speech where he told a story that put his final message in context. The wrap-up might be where you tie up your 'top and tail', referring back to a point you mentioned at the start so you can then link it to your message.

Your final message

And now it's time! Time for your final message. So, face the audience. You can indicate to your audience that you know it's the end, by taking a breath. Or pausing. Or saying something like, 'To wrap up,' 'In conclusion' or 'Here's what to do next'. This sets their mind up for your memorable statement.

Your Message Statement now has a uniting power. It coalesces all your information into a satisfying, recallable, transferable summary. The *ending message* helps the audience see the logical flow of your information and it ties your presentation up with a bow.

OPTIONAL TECHNIQUES TO ENGAGE YOUR LISTENERS

The techniques to further engage your audience are grouped into 3 areas. You can use them to:

- **Provoke** the mind of your listener
- **Connect** with your listener
- **Activate** the mind of your listener.

© 2002 Ted Goff

"Did you skip over the interesting parts of your talk on purpose?"

How to PROVOKE the mind of your listener

Here are my favourite ways to provoke the listener's mind to ensure they're engaged.

[a] You may be thinking …

The first is called the *'You may be thinking...'* technique (YMBT). It counters objections or concerns that may block the absorption of your ideas. Many speakers are relieved when they finish their presentation without anyone from the audience asking them difficult questions.

This is a fool's paradise. Most people who have concerns don't mention them. Research shows, that for every person who complains about a product or service, there are 19 others who were unhappy but chose not to say anything. In other words, only 1 in 20 people will speak up.

It's the same with your audience. Most people who have concerns or objections that might make them resist your ideas, won't say anything. But these unaddressed concerns can kill your project. Your listeners need their objections neutralised. This technique raises the concern and then satisfies it with a reasonable response. Here's how to use it: work out the questions or concerns your audience might have, then state them like this:

> *"You may be thinking... [state their question or concern. Then state your response]"*.

When this technique is done well, your question provokes their mind, then satisfies it with your answer. Below is a form you can use to 1) write down the question or concern *in the language the audience would use,* and 2) write your response.

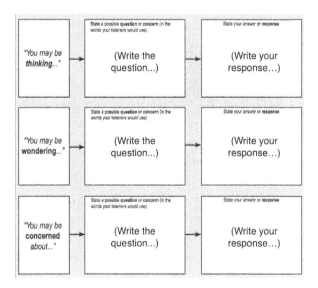

Here's an example of how it might sound:

> *"You may be thinking, the price is too high. Well, that's a common concern, but when you factor in the life of the product, it's actually more cost effective than the alternatives."*

Benefits to the YMBT technique

Here's a machine-gun list of benefits for the 'you may be thinking technique'. It demonstrates you understand their perspective, building trust as a result. It dissolves objections, making people more open to your message. It creates a 'dialogue feel'. Your presentation feels 2-way rather than one-way. This is more engaging. It reduces the cognitive effort required by the listener to explore the idea, so you are easier to listen to. It builds commitment. They feel more satisfied the ideas have been explored objectively, and you'll never be surprised by a question on stage, because you've identified them beforehand.

[b] Metaphors

A good metaphor paints a rich picture in just a few words. It's a figure of speech or a comparison, where a word or phrase ordinarily used for one thing, is applied to another. In it's most basic form it works like this:

A [first thing] is a [second thing].

For example, 'life is a roller coaster'. Well, it's not *actually* a roller coaster, but it might feel like it sometimes. The metaphor adds a strong emotional and visual image to the idea. And it *provokes* the mind into action by compelling your listener to *make* a comparison.

Metaphors are a great way to see a subject from a different angle, or express an idea in a vivid way. Metaphors engage the mind because when you compare 2 unlike things, you create mental images in the mind of the listener *automatically*. What an amazing power to have! With a few words you force activity in the mind of another person.

We've seen how the coach of Hawthorn Football Club used metaphor, describing the opposing team as a 'shark' which will 'die' if it stops moving. This was a powerful way of getting across the idea of relentless tackling to 'kill' the other team's game plan.

Einstein became the most famous person of the 20th century, not just because he was smart, but because he was able to communicate complex ideas in simple ways. He often used metaphor to do this. For example, when asked his opinion on the new theory of quantum physics, he rejected it with, *"God does not play dice with the universe"*. When talking about the atrocities of war, he said, *"Technological progress is like an axe in the hands of a pathological criminal."* And when he wanted to get across a point about crowd thinking he said, *"In order to form an immaculate member of a flock of sheep, one must, above all, be a sheep"*.

Einstein also used metaphor to simplify new ideas. Here he is explaining the new technology of the day:

> *"You see, wire telegraph is a kind of a very, very long cat. You pull his tail in New York and his head is meowing in Los Angeles. Do you understand this? And radio operates exactly the same way: you send signals here, they receive them there. The only difference is that there is no cat."*

Here's another Steve Jobs example. After launching the new iPad tablet, Jobs was asked if tablets would succeed the laptop. He responded,

> *"When we were an agrarian nation, all cars were trucks, because that's what you needed on the farm. But as vehicles started to be used in the urban centres, cars got more popular. Innovations like automatic transmission and power steering and things that you didn't care about in a truck as much started to become paramount in cars. PCs (personal computers) are going to be like trucks. They're still going to be around, they're still going to have a lot of value, but they're going to be used by 1 out of X people."*

So, laptop and desktop computers are 'trucks', and tablets are 'cars' that are easier to use.

Props as metaphor

I use a prop as a metaphor. It's a simple red ball. I tell people the red ball is their message. When I throw it to someone in the audience I tell them it represents the speaker transferring a message to the listener. Then, I ask the person who caught it, to throw the ball to someone else in the audience. This represents the message being transferred to others.

This simple prop gets an idea across quickly and with great recall. We even used the metaphor in our logo.

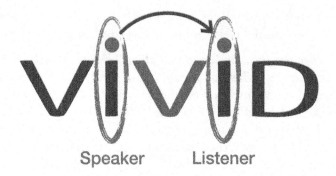

I'm sharing this with you so you can see how to develop your own metaphors. The red ball came about because I went through the exercise of saying, 'A message is like...' ...well, it's like a thing flying through the air between the speaker and the listener, um, like throwing and catching a ball.

All you need to do is say the following out loud and maybe brainstorm it with friends...

> *"This [project, idea, challenge, etc] is like..."*

...and see if you can come up with a kick-ass metaphor to embed in the mind of your audience.

[c] Imagine…

Here's another technique Einstein liked - he explained a theory about the fact that nothing is faster than the speed of light, by saying:

> *"Imagine you are driving a car in space at the speed of light: what happens if you turn the headlights on?"*

This is a metaphor with a boost - the word 'imagine'. He brought a difficult concept to a level most audiences could understand and retain. The 'imagine technique' is another way of provoking the mind of your listener. It transports your listeners into 'the picture'. I call these images 'imagine scenarios' or 'living examples'. There are a number of ways to use 'imagine scenarios'. Here are just a few:

- Imagine… [paint a picture of the future].

- Imagine… [outline the positive result if we do X]
- Imagine… [outline the negative result if we don't]
- Imagine… [the problem solved]
- Imagine… [experiencing these good/bad feelings]

Guiding people through an *imagine scenario* makes them feel part of the story rather than just observers of it. That's why the *imagine... technique* is used all the time in advertising. However, we can also learn from advertisers who use it poorly. It's not a matter of just throwing in the word 'imagine'. Remember to paint the picture for them. So, rather than saying, "Imagine the benefits of having more time…", say:

> *"Imagine what you could do with an extra hour per day.... write that novel, play more golf, relax more instead of rushing, etc."*

Notice the imagery? Another example: instead of saying, "Imagine being able to call the USA for just 35 cents per minute", say:

> *"Imagine chatting to your family more often. Imagine seeing the small number on your phone bill and realising you can call your friends in the USA for not much more than calling interstate."*

Instead of, "Imagine the speed of broadband internet", say,

> *"Imagine sitting at your computer and have pages load instantly as you click. No more waiting for pages to load..."*

Get it? Great. Have fun with it.

How to CONNECT with your listener

Stories are a powerful way to connect with your listener. A good way to build your storytelling skills is to start with simple *examples*, then add some *memory hooks* and finally some vivid 'story' *components*.

[a] Examples

Language is imprecise and the meaning of a word depends on context. Examples put things into a specific context and make your points more concrete. They transform the vague into the specific. Examples also help your listeners see an issue from *their* perspective. Most presentations have too much data and too few examples.

A simple way to craft your own examples is to imagine a listener saying to you: "Give me an example from real life." "Give me an example of how it would work." "Explain how my role would be affected." "Give me an example of the problem." "Give me an example of the benefit." ...and so on.

Testimonials: Sometimes called 'social proof', testimonials are often examples told in somebody else's voice. They can be very powerful. You might read someone's testimonial-example or play a video of it.

[b] Memory hooks

Vivid examples usually include 'memory hooks'. What's a memory hook you ask? Think of the listener's mind as a smooth wall. Words and ideas might touch the mind, but slide off. Memory hooks connect with something *already in the audience's mind*. It's like a hook that pulls your example deeper into their awareness. Memory hooks are references to familiar places or situations we can all relate to, like:

- Common life experiences (school, marriage, summer holidays, etc)
- Relationships (mother, father, sister, brother, best friend, boss, etc.)
- Movies, TV, music and other popular culture
- Famous people, famous events
- Locations (The city the conference is in, a familiar landmark)
- Brand names ('I grabbed the Dyson to clean up the pretzels')
You get the idea...

Hooks can also be expressed as physical movement – you act out a 'common life experience' like digging for a phone that's lost at the bottom of your bag, or clicking a mouse frantically in frustration at a slow-loading web page. Connecting with your audience this way makes your topic seem more familiar, and it's easier for people to feel involved in your subject.

Paul Kelly's classic song from 1987, *To her door* is loaded with memory hooks. In fact, it's *chockas*. The song's lyrics are a great example of painting a vivid picture; a compelling story in just 178 words. Here are the lyrics with memory hooks in bold.

They got **married** early, never **had no money.**
Then when he **got laid off** they really **hit the skids.**
He started up his **drinking**, then they started **fighting.**
He **took it pretty badly**, she took both **the kids.**
She said: "I'm not **standing by**, to watch you slowly **die.**
So watch me **walking, out the door**".
She said, "Shove it, Jack, I'm **walking out the door**".

She **went to her brother's**, got a little **bar work.**
He went to **the Buttery[rehab clinic]**, stayed about a year.
Then he **wrote a letter**, said "**I want to see you**".
She thought he sounded better, she **sent him up the fare.**
He was **riding** through **the cane** in the **pouring rain.**
On **Olympic[bus]** to **her door.**

He came in on a **Sunday**, every **muscle aching.**
Walking in slow motion like he'd **just been hit.**
Did they have a future? Would he know his **children**?
Could he make a picture and get them all to fit?
He was **shaking in his seat** riding through **the streets.**
In a **silver-top[taxi]** to **her door.**
(Songwriters: KELLY, PAUL MAURICE, To Her Door lyrics © Sony/ATV Music Publishing LLC, Warner/Chappell Music, Inc.)

Next time you craft an example, see if you can include some memory hooks to help bring your example to life.

[c] Story components

Have you ever listened to a bad storyteller? It's frustrating. A typical bad story is a series of facts held together by 'and then …', 'and then …' , 'and then …'. The simplest way to make your story interesting is to have a point. But you can do much better.

The top 3 components of a vivid story

Predetermined story structures can sometimes be too rigid. The solution? Master the *components* of great storytelling, so you can build a vivid story to suit your needs. Here are 3 components of a compelling story.

1. Set the scene

Introduce the situation and paint a picture of the scene. For example, where did the events happen? Is there a backstory to your main story? Set it up. Then, add your characters (and maybe exaggerate their qualities a little). For example:

> *'It happened in this room! Seven people sitting around the boardroom table with the CEO screaming across the mahogany in anger, and the Sales Manager red faced trying to defend his position...'*

2. Paint a picture of the characters

Defining your characters can make your story pop. What can you tell us about your characters? Name? Role? Personality style? Is the character shy, loud, ditzy, a close talker, a soft talker, etc. Listeners invest emotionally in well-painted characters. You don't even have to go into great detail, doesn't this one line tell you a lot about the person?

> *'My dad was so loud you could hear him singing from all the way down the street.'*

When I tell stories about communication, I often start with my parents.

> *'My parents confused me from a young age. When I asked a question, Mum never gave enough information and Dad always gave too much. Mum would simplify so much that I didn't learn anything and Dad would overwhelm me with so many details (and diagrams written on the back of a cigarette packet!) that I never wanted to ask another question.'*

Now I can continue with a story and my listeners will be interested in how each character acts or *reacts* to a situation. They are invested, interested in what happens to these people.

Another thing you can do to build your character is get more specific about an aspect of their appearance or personality. For example:

> 'Ralph has a stooped posture like he's been carrying a weight his whole life.'

> 'The founder of Smoogle had a little notebook and pen in his top pocket every day of his working life. He was determined to catch all his brilliant ideas and never waste a useful thought.'

> 'My sales manager is never still. He always has something in his hands, like a cricket ball or a pen, and is constantly clicking his fingers.'

Don't you want to know what happens to these characters in a story now that you know a bit about them?

3. Enhance the drama!

When my son was six years old, he came home from school and said proudly, "Today I wrote my *own* story". As I started to ask him about it, he jumped in excitedly and said, "And Daddy, a story has to have a problem and a solution." I said, "Cool. What was your story about?"
"I was flying a kite."
"What was the problem?" I asked.
"The string broke."
"Bummer. What happened next?"
"A man came and fixed it." End of story!

I giggled inside at the simplicity of his story, but later realised that his kite escapade taught him a crucial lesson that many speakers still don't understand. Drama. Where is the drama in your story?

Ask yourself: What are the important events? What are the stakes? Is there tension and resolution? Were you up against a deadline? Was there a turning point that threw your plan into disarray? Drama comes from the following areas:

Events: What are the dramatic events in your story? Isolate significant events from details. Cinderella meeting the fairy godmother, the carriage turning back into a pumpkin at midnight, and the prince seeing that the shoe fits Cinderella, are all dramatic events. Cinderella sweeping the floor is not.

Obstacles: What obstacles are encountered as you (or your character) attempt to achieve a goal.

Stakes: High stakes build suspense. What bad thing will happen if you fail? In movies like *Ghostbusters*, *Armageddon* and *Independence Day*, the 'bad thing' is that the earth will be destroyed. What bad thing will happen if your project fails?

Countdown: People can't resist a countdown or a deadline, it's like a ticking time bomb. How many days to the deadline? For example, the race is tomorrow and their car is in pieces all over the garage, or our heroes have to get on the plane in the next 2 minutes because the villains are chasing them.

Conflict: Are there arguments between team members? Is there a villain? (The police chief says to the rogue detective, "The Mayor called me personally to ensure you stay off this case - or I'll have your badge!"). Internal conflict is also compelling. Self doubt is conflict. Were you about to give up? Did you feel like the opposing forces had beaten you? Did you worry that you didn't have it in you to succeed? Remember; *'that which is most personal is most universal'*. Consider sharing your doubts and concerns with your audience.

Turning point: At a turning point, the story goes in a new direction. Perhaps a character has had a revelation or they've made a difficult decision. Maybe they have learnt vital information or set a new goal. A turning point implies language like: "...and that's when I realised..." or "...then came the breakthrough..." So, what did you realise? What was the breakthrough in your story?

Climax: Obstacles, stakes, suspense, countdowns, conflict and turning points all build to your climax, which is simply the satisfying ending to your story.

You now have a feel for the 3 key elements of a compelling story.

1) Setting the scene,

2) Painting a picture of your characters, and

3) Adding drama.

And the great thing for a speech or presentation is, you don't need to put them all together and craft a 2-hour screenplay or 400-page novel. Your 'stories' can be tiny scenes that use just 1 or 2 of these elements. You don't need to cram them all in.

For example, my 'Skate Park story' earlier on in the book uses 3 story elements: characters (me, 15 year old skaters, someone's mum and a nurse), 2 x high stakes events (knocking myself out on the skate ramp, uncontrollable shaking at the hospital) and 1 x revelation (there is a separation between your ability to think and physical symptoms). The end.

Choose the story *elements* that work in your situation, and then use them as building blocks. Cherry-picking story *elements* helps shorten or lengthen the story to fit the time you have allocated.

How to tell your story

If you want to learn from the best, watch standup comedians. They are usually great storytellers. In a short amount of time they set the scene, reveal their characters, bring the drama to life and highlight a turning point or punchline. Don't worry, you don't have to be as good as a professional comedian, but it is important to *commit* to your story.

See if you can inhabit a character - mimic their voice, style or movement. You don't have to be an actor or an extrovert. Do it simply to express your character's uniqueness.

For example, if you're in marketing and you're talking about your target market - *a professional woman aged 28-32 years who only listens to radio in her car*. Be her, while you are talking about her. Give her a name, say Daphne, and say "Imagine I'm Daphne ..." Hold the imaginary steering wheel, adjust the volume button on the radio. Not overacting in a pantomime-style, just move the way you would hold the wheel if you were driving.

Take away point

You don't have to be brilliant at every story component. You do need to give your audience a satisfying ending. And in most cases this is simply the takeaway point.

How to ACTIVATE your listener's mind

Here are a few simple options to activate the mind of your listener.

[a] Contrast

Howard Hughes inherited a fortune at age 19 and moved to Hollywood to make his name as a filmmaker. He produced and directed *Hells Angels* in 1930, which is considered one of the first big budget action films. It's about combat pilots in World War 1 and contains the most incredible dogfight sequences ever filmed.

During filming however, Hughes had a problem. The planes were flying dangerously fast but there was nothing in the background but sky, so it didn't *seem* fast. With no contrast it was impossible to get a sense of how fast the planes were going.

Hughes realised he needed clouds in the background. Unfortunately, he couldn't just add them with CGI graphics as filmmakers do today. So he decided to wait for clouds and *reshoot* the entire flying sequences. But the weather was so good around Hollywood it was difficult to find clouds! He hired a full-time meteorologist whose sole job was to predict where to find clouds, with enough warning so the crew could get to that location for filming. There was a lot of waiting around and it put the film way over budget, but it worked. Contrast helped the audience see the reality of the plane's speed - a fact that was unclear without contrast. The movie was a hit and made money even though its budget blew out to a massive $3.8 million (by far the most expensive movie ever made at the time).

Life is rife with opposing forces: light/dark; hot/cold; male/female; black/white; life/death, up/down. When you think about it, all forces exist in opposition in a way that helps frame our understanding of the world we live in. Our mind's are activated by contrast. Contrast is also great for highlighting both sides of an argument, which helps the mind retain and recall an idea. Contrast is an easy technique to use. The simplest way is to say what something is NOT. For example,

"This product is poor at X, however if you want Y it's the best."

"This project won't do A, but it will give us B."

"If you want the cheapest product on the market, then forget about product X, however, if you want the best, this is the answer."

Showing contrasting viewpoints helps your ideas emerge from the background. Using contrast makes a stronger impression than just emphasising benefits.

The language of contrast

Imagine you're making a presentation about a new direction for your company. Instead of just saying: "This strategy will take us in the right direction to achieve our goals", say…

"If we keep going in this direction we will end up with X... (bad stuff)...however, with the new strategy we will end up with Y... (good stuff)."

Here's another example of the language of contrast. Instead of saying: "Sales are 1.3 million". Refer to the past to show contrast. You might say,

"2 years ago we had sales of $400K... now we have sales of $1.3 million."

You might even use your hands to demonstrate contrast. Holding out your left hand you say something like, "In the past...", then, holding out your right hand, you say, "But now...".

As always, you don't need to be a professional actor or force the gesture. Imagine you're explaining these ideas at a desk to one person if that helps you feel more comfortable. These techniques can be just as appropriate in normal conversation.

[b] Variation

No matter what speaking style you have, loud or quiet, fast or slow, if it is *unchanging*, it can become tedious to your listeners. Variety engages. You already have the chunk structure to provide some variation, which is a good start - as you open and close each chunk, you provide variety. However, there are many options to provide variation when you speak.

Movement: Consider walking to different points on the stage to add variation, it forces the audience to follow you with their eyes. Or use your hands to emphasise points.

Interactivity: Give the audience an exercise. Like catching a 'message ball' or turning to a certain page of your handout. Ask the audience questions - either rhetorical questions or direct questions where you want them to answer.

Pace: Play with your pace. Most people speak more quickly than they need to. Learning to slow down is a good starting point. However, variation is the key. A long silence can have a strong impact.

Volume: Think of your voice as having a volume control from 1-10. You'll have a comfortable range (usually a narrow range). Play with it. Start by going to the opposite of your natural range just 10% of the time. Perhaps as you make a point. You'll quickly be able to expand your range.

Your effortless vocal range

In the past I was a 'try-er'. I know this because my Alexander Teacher used this term as an insult to help me learn an important lesson. "You're one of those 'try-ers' Cam", she said in a disparaging tone. What was the lesson she was teaching me? It was about *wasted effort*. When I spoke to an audience, I tried *so hard* to be impressive, using so much effort to speak, I was wearing out my vocal cords.

What's an 'Alexander Teacher' you ask? It's someone who instructs on body awareness to improve performance. The idea is to use the 'self' more effectively. Many dancers, singers, musicians, actors and athletes have benefited from the Alexander Technique, which guides us on how to use our body with reduced effort.

The reason I was visiting her twice a week was that I was losing my voice on stage. It was painful, frustrating and had me second-guessing my career choice of professional speaker and trainer. My Alexander Teacher explained that our voice doesn't 'wear out' if we use it properly. She also explained that speaking in a relaxed way, without all the trying and over-efforting, might even engage the audience more effectively.

You don't need to exhaust yourself

Initially, this was difficult to accept. I played football and was taught that we needed to use 150% effort and have 200% commitment! Have nothing left at the end of a game. No pain, no gain! So, I guess it just felt normal to exhaust myself when speaking for high stakes.

When I first attempted to speak with 'no effort' it just didn't feel right. I assumed the audience would think I didn't care about what I was saying. I kept falling back into my long-standing rhythm of FULL VOLUME ALL THE TIME. The breakthrough was learning to whisper on stage. My teacher said, 'From now on, every time you make an important point you must whisper it.'

Now, it's not as quiet as a real whisper, but it does take me from a volume level of 9-out-of-10, down to 4-out-of-10. This technique gave me an awareness of **vocal variation**, which I've been able to refine over time. When I think back to how much I used to exhaust myself during a speech, it's mind blowing. I found I didn't need to tense every muscle when speaking, as I attempted to reach 200% effort. As Jedi Master Yoda famously said to Luke Skywalker, "Do. Or do not. There is no *try*."

The whisper technique

The whisper technique has worked for many of my clients as well. For example, Jules Lund has a powerful presence, but found vocal variety difficult. On a scale of 1-10 Jules was also at 9 or 10 most of the time. That was ok as a TV presenter on shows like Getaway, where he spoke for 10 seconds and then the camera cut to a beautiful location or an interview with a local. But Jules was about to make a 60 minute presentation at a Radio Conference. An hour of speaking at an intensity of 9-out-of-10 would not only wear Jules' voice out, it would wear out the audience.

Once again, the whisper technique proved to be the trigger that helped him to have more control and variety when presenting. If you think this scenario matches your style, give the whisper technique a go.

The Power of the Pause

An 'extrovert-style' speaker tends to speak loudly. Getting an extrovert style from a volume level of 10 down to a level of 5 using the whisper technique gives great vocal variety. However, what if you're more of an introvert style and your voice rarely gets above 5-out-of-10? Should you scream to add vocal variety?

Probably not. The technique for you to master is **pausing**.

Pausing has many benefits for both the speaker and the audience. It gives your audience space to process and embed your ideas. And it gives you time to breathe, gather your thoughts and regroup throughout the talk. A pause can set up an important point. Pausing allows a point to stand out and sink in. You just need the ability to shut your mouth for 3 or 4 seconds after you make it!

The foundation for pausing is also built into the chunk structure. It shows you *where* to pause - like a trusted friend guiding you through the speech. When you think of a speech in *sections*, where you introduce and wrap-up each section, you'll start to pause naturally.

[c] Emphasis

Emphasis is similar to variation, but worth looking at separately. Variation is a *general principle* about varying the energy in the room, whereas *emphasis* requires the identification of *what* to emphasise. When you know what you want to emphasise, it will start to happen automatically, so it also flows automatically with your structure and key points. Other methods of achieving emphasis include:

Wording: Use language to signpost important ideas. For example, hook them with lines like, "You may want to make a note of this…" or "This next point may be of particular interest to you…" or "And this is a crucial point…" Sometimes I just let out a 'Boom!' after a killer point.

Rich words: The 'insanely great' Steve Jobs used to drop words like groundbreaking, game-changer, amazing, staggering and insanely great. I remember being enthralled by a speaker who used 'diabolical' and 'preposterous' in the same sentence. 'It's a diabolical problem but the current solution is preposterous...' We all wanted to hear *her* solution!

Chunks: The START and END of *anything* will capture people's attention. Even if they're daydreaming or looking at their phones while you speak, your audience will stop and focus on you when you indicate you are starting or ending a *section*. This is amazingly powerful. For example, indicate you are STARTING a section by saying; "Now, let's move on to..." or "Next, lets have a look at..." or even, "Secondly...", etc.

Or, demonstrate you're ENDING a section and they won't be able to look away! For example. "The key point here is..." or "Just to wrap up..." or "In summary..." or "So, what does that mean to you?...", etc.

Great explanations give you effortless delivery skills

Have you noticed that none of these techniques requires a particular style? They are optional and flexible. They adapt to *your* style. They don't paint you into a corner by requiring specific body language. They simply help bring your information to life.

Giving great explanations will boost your delivery skills with very little effort. And help both you and your audience enjoy the experience!

VISUAL EXPLANATIONS - LEVERAGING SLIDES AND VISUAL SUPPORT

Before we discuss slides, PowerPoint and presentation software, let's take a moment to look at visual support from a broader perspective. Your goal with visual support is to make your information easier to follow and easier to remember - or to bring an idea to life.

When I speak to a small group sitting at a table, I usually have a yellow notepad and a pen. I write key words and I scribble wonky diagrams. Then I flick the page over and do it some more. These scribbles add tremendous visual support to my explanations.

The equivalent of this is to use a flip-chart or whiteboard during a presentation. The flip chart is a fantastic, yet underused presentation tool. It's main strength is that the image is created by you *as you speak*.

The sliding scale

Don't think about PowerPoint first, think about visual devices that will help people understand your ideas. For example, a great visual device is the 'sliding scale' which can be used on a slide, a flip chart or created in the air with your arms. It seems that many people see the world in black and white. *Are you an introvert or an extrovert? Are you a democrat or a republican? Are you an optimist or a pessimist? Do you suffer from public speaking anxiety or not? What's more important, body language or words?*

An accurate answer is often, 'It depends...'. The simple sliding scale can help break people's thinking out of rigid and unhelpful limitations. So, what is a sliding scale? It's just a line showing extremes.

One extreme--Other extreme

This simple diagram can help people open their mind and see an issue from a different perspective. For example:

Extrovert---Introvert

Some people are extreme extroverts or introverts, while others are closer to the middle of the scale.

The sliding scale also gives you a visual reference to answer questions. For example, I'm often asked whether some people are 'hopeless cases' and will never be good speakers, no matter how much training they receive. I always use the sliding scale to answer that question.

Terrible--Amazing

I point out that even if they're terrible now, message and structure will move them along the line, *closer* to amazing. They may never be totally amazing, but clear and memorable is so much better than 'terrible'.

Terrible----->--------->-------Clear----------------------------Amazing

Two-by-two grid

A two-by-two grid is an example of a visual model to convey ideas. For example, when Steve Jobs returned to Apple in 1997 they were 30 days from bankruptcy. He refocused the company with a simple quadrant scribbled on a whiteboard.

At the time, Apple was producing a dozen different versions of the Macintosh. After a few weeks attending product review sessions, Jobs had had enough. Producing such a large number of options was not only scattering their limited resources, he realised it was a communication problem. Jobs asked his team, "Why would I recommend a 3400 model over a 4400? When should somebody jump up to a 6500 model, but not a 7300? Which Mac should I recommend to my friends?"

He recognised that if he couldn't figure it out working inside Apple with all these experts advising him, how were customers going make decisions? So, during a meeting he stopped the discussion, grabbed a Magic Marker and drew a two-by-two grid. "Here's what we need," he declared.

He labeled the 2 *columns*, 'Consumer' and 'Pro'. He labeled the *rows* 'Desktop' and 'Notebook'.

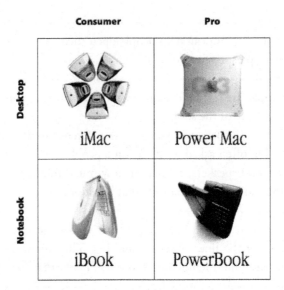

There would only be 2 categories of Apple computer, desktop and notebook. And each category had 2 varieties: consumer and pro. This visual model focused everyone.

He told his team to build 4 great products, 1 for each quadrant. All other products were canceled. There was a stunned silence as people digested the enormity of the change. But by getting Apple to focus on making just 4 computers, he saved the company. In 1998 he used the same two-by-two grid on stage to launch Apple's streamlined offerings to the world.

Do you even need visual support?

Of course, you don't have to use visual support at all (I'll explore a Jim Collins speech with no visuals in a few pages), but when you do, realise there are *many ways* to engage people - whether it's a flip chart, slides or just using your hands to draw a diagram in the air.

Even though there are many ways to provide visual support, most of the questions I receive are about *slides*. So, here are **4 principles** to help you leverage presentation software.

Principle 1: Choose your presentation software

Even though there are many presentation software options, the principles for engaging your audience with visual support are the same whether you use PowerPoint, Apple's Keynote or Prezi.

I prefer Keynote at the moment, but my clients use all three. The differences are predominantly in the creation tools. If you think about it, once you're on stage, the main function of all presentation software is simply to move from one image or slide to the next. So the best presentation software is the one *you* prefer to use to *create* your slides.

The current winner in the hype stakes is Prezi. Some people argue that the zooming nature of Prezi makes it fundamentally different from Keynote and PowerPoint for your audience. But is it fundamentally different? Well, it depends on your goals.

Prezi and LucidChart

Prezi is a cloud-based program that doesn't work on the traditional slide metaphor. The result is considered more dynamic than PowerPoint or Keynote because of its *zooming user interface.*

What's a zooming user interface, you ask?

Your presentation is laid out on a large virtual canvas, not slides, and you zoom in and out of a particular area in order to see more detail or less detail. Like the way Google Maps lets you zoom into a street, then back out to the view of the city.

So instead of appearing like a progression of slides, the audience feels like they are zooming in and out of text, images, videos, charts, etc. In fact, Prezi calls it a 'map', not slides, and your presentation zooms in and out of your map to show relationships between information.

Prezi was created by a Hungarian architect who wanted to be able to zoom in on his designs to show the detail of a room, then zoom out to show the bigger picture. So Prezi is great at achieving that visual goal.

LucidChart.com is another option. It's great for creating online flowcharts and diagrams and uses the same kind of virtual canvas to lay out elements of a presentation. It has an easy-to-use 'presentation mode' that also allows you to zoom in and out of different areas.

But as I see it, the zooming is just an animation feature. Nothing wrong with that, of course. In fact, I particularly like Prezi to zoom into *stage 1* of a flowchart, then zoom out to see all the stages, then back into the detail of stage 2, and so on. And if you like MindMapping, you'll probably be thrilled with Prezi or LucidChart. They can also add energy and movement to your visuals in the same way zooming TV cameras fly into and away from a contestant on 'The Voice' or 'Who Wants to Be A Millionaire'.

However, many people think, 'It's not PowerPoint, so I'll avoid the death by PowerPoint syndrome'. Sorry, it's not that easy. I remember hearing the same hopeful cries 10 years ago when companies employed FLASH animators to put their presentations together. If you haven't nailed the message and structure, no software tool will save you.

And remember, you don't want compliments about your animations – you want people talking about your ideas! Make your decisions around graphics and presentation software based on their ability to illuminate your ideas.

Principle 2: Change your relationship with the screen

Winston Smith, the protagonist in George Orwell's book *Nineteen Eighty-four'* lived in the world of Big Brother where huge *tele-screens* delivering government propaganda were in every home, workplace and public space. And they were always *on*. They couldn't be turned off, even at home.

One day Winston has a meeting in the office of an inner party official. As they start their discussion, the party official clicks a button and *turns the screen off*. Winston is stunned. "You can turn it off?!"he says in wide-eyed amazement. His expression is a cross between a starving man being given food, and a slave being released from his chains.

What does this have to do with business presentations? Ask yourself, why is that presentation screen behind the speaker *always* on? Wouldn't the images have more impact if the screen was blank some of the time?

The answer is yes. You see, the fundamental problem that leads to 'death by PowerPoint' is not the technology, it's how the presenter uses it. The speaker makes the presentation, and the slides are support.

Too often presentation software is seen as the master. People even refer to their slide deck or PowerPoint file as 'the presentation'. Have you seen this before: the speaker stands on a spot next to the screen. Hardly moving. Reading the words. It seems that if the slide didn't appear, the speaker wouldn't have a clue what to say.

The 'B' key

A great way to take control of your presentation software is to use the 'B' key on the keyboard, which *blacks out the screen*. I'm constantly amazed at how few people even know about the 'B' key function. Only 10% of business presenters use this blank screen effect.

Are you wondering how you return to your slides after the screen goes blank? Simply press the B key again. Most remotes have a button for this function. This simple technique improves your presentation in many ways. Here are 7 specific benefits of the B key.

Benefit 1: It changes the relationship you have with PowerPoint

Knowing you have the power to blank the screen reduces the chance you'll use the presentation software as a crutch. The simple act of switching your slides on and off *as needed* can change your mindset. You *choose* to have it on – or off.

Benefit 2: It helps you start thinking more creatively

Your mindset can completely change, you start to ask yourself great questions like: 'Do I need a slide here? Will it help my audience understand? Or should I just tell a story?' You might even move to a whiteboard or flip-chart to write a key word or draw a wonky diagram.

Benefit 3: You look more impressive

Most speakers look uncertain about the technology they're using. When you hit the 'B' key and you know that you have control over the technology it changes the entire experience for you and positively impacts your audience's perception of you.

Benefit 4: It makes it easier for your audience to digest information

Blanking the screen helps create structure for the audience. This makes it easier for audiences to focus, compared to one, long unbroken presentation. It also improves the effect of stories and examples - or when you show an object, prop, handout or product. For example, you can use your slides to stay on track and then you blank the screen and say, "Let me tell you a story that illustrates this point". You finish the story, bring the slides back, and continue.

Benefit 5: It changes the mood of the room. Dramatically

The audience gets variation and emphasis, which keeps energy levels up. We fall asleep while the TV is on, but as soon as someone turns it off, you wake up. Each time the screen goes on or off, people are drawn to the stage. The human mind can't resist the start or the end of something. It's fantastic if you want to deliver a critical point.

Benefit 6: It gives you more flexibility

When you want to go off topic or step away from planned material, it will help you control the impromptu discussion without distraction. If there are questions, you can blank the screen and focus on their query. When the audience sees you engage thoughtfully with one person, they feel closer to you too.

Benefit 7: It is the perfect way to end with impact

Hit the "B" key. Pause. And deliver your message. Boom!

Principle 3: Design your slides

Think billboards, not magazine ads

One way to produce good visuals is to think of them as billboards as opposed to magazine ads. Billboard messages need to be able to be absorbed quickly and easily from a distance as drivers zoom by. As a result, the good ones contain a bare minimum of words, presented in large, easy to read fonts with high contrast. In other words, you glance at billboards while you're focused on something else, like a presentation.

Magazine ads, however are read alone. You give your full attention to them. You don't have someone explaining them to you. The simple principle of *slides as billboards* can guide your thinking and help you produce effective visual aids.

Avoid full sentences

Why do speakers fill their slides with full sentences? Usually for one of these reasons: 1) They're worried about forgetting something. 2) Their slides will be passed on as handouts or emails after the presentation and won't make sense without full sentences. 3) They believe that more information on the slides shows more research done on the presentation. 4) Everyone else in the organisation does it that way.

Let's look at each of these reasons.

First, each person needs to decide for themselves how to manage their notes. Some people don't need any and are happy to talk to a few images or speak from memory. Others want to use their slides to keep them on track. However, reading full sentences doesn't achieve the goal. Reading can shut down your ability to think freely. And they confuse the audience, who get caught between trying to listen to what you are saying and reading off the screen. The best solution is to reduce the number of words on the screen. You can still use notes as a prompt if you need them, but use your notes to form the sentences yourself rather than reading off the screen. This will keep your brain active and bring the ideas to life more effectively.

Second, a good document makes a poor slide, just as a well designed slide makes a poor document. Trying to achieve both at once will see you fail on both counts. Are you creating a document or a slide? They are different animals. Slides are support to a speaker, while a document needs to convey all the information on its own.

Third, in some corporate cultures, the idea of having no slides, few slides or not much on the slides, is taken as a sign that you haven't done much research. In other words, throwing more mud on the screen shows how much mud you have been swimming in to prepare this talk (mud equals data in this analogy). So, a lot of people are trying to show that they're serious and committed to a project by the amount of stuff that they can cram onto their slides. Don't fall for this.

Fourth, *"If your mate Joe put his head in the fire, should you put your head in the fire too?"* (When I was a kid, my dad offered this Yoda-like wisdom every time I wasn't allowed to do something my friends were doing.) Just because your colleagues follow a cluttered slide design, doesn't mean you should too.

Sometimes full sentences on slides make sense though. It's not a rule, it's a guideline. For example, when speaking to an audience in another country or posting slides online. A Vietnamese speaker at a recent conference in Singapore was talking to an audience containing people from the Philippines, Germany, Indonesia, China and Korea. The presentation was in English but the speaker and everybody in the audience had English as their second language. In this case, slides with full sentences (albeit short sentences) were more effective at conveying ideas and developing understanding in the audience.

Bullet points are OK

You might be surprised to read that bullet points are ok. Some good books like *Presentation Zen* argue that bullet points are bad and we should use more images and much less text. Well, this is a good way to go, but it's not the *only* way to go. Bullet points work fine if you verbally bring them to life. Of course, the flip side is also true, your beautiful graphic design won't have much impact if you don't explain it effectively.

The essence of Zen design is clean and simple with lots of space and *nothing* added that doesn't have a purpose. This trend towards simplicity is a good one. Some people still feel the need to fill all gaps with something, but just like using too many words to get a message across, the more you leave out, the stronger the remaining message becomes.

As always, design fashions can change and people's preferences will vary. Ultimately, slide design is up to you. And even though bullet points have had bad press, the traditional slide format with a heading and bullet points can be effective when used well. Just don't pack too many bullets onto a slide, use the minimum number of words you need to reinforce the point, include images and diagrams when you can (and maybe blank the screen from time to time using the 'B' key).

Your company logo on every slide?

Good designs tend to have plenty of empty space. Design is not decoration. Who says your logo should be on every slide?! Branding is an often misunderstood term. For example, sticking your logo on every slide is less effective at branding than leaving a branding message in the mind of your audience.

Having your logo on the first and last slide is more effective than putting it on every slide. Why? Because the logo doesn't help you make a point, but it will clutter your slides, adding to the 'noise' and reducing your credibility. How does this reduce your credibility? It makes your presentation look commercial, and we know that people trust *editorial* content and they distrust advertising content.

So by adding logos all through your presentation, you make it look like an ad, not an editorial-style explanation. We don't begin every new sentence of a conversation restating our name.

Quote marks can double the impact of a point

Quotes from other people are very powerful. There's something about the third-party credibility that makes them pop. It's not you saying it, it's them supporting your argument.

How many slides per minute?

I'm regularly asked questions like, 'How many slides per minute is optimum', or 'How long should each slide be up on the screen?' I have no answer because it's the wrong way to approach visual support. It depends on the slide. A flow chart or diagram may be on screen for five minutes as you explain different parts of it. Text slides would ideally not be up long.

It's OK to swim in the light of the projector

One of the presentation 'rules' out there is that you shouldn't cast a shadow on the screen. Sure, this is good advice if you are annoyingly standing in front of your slides with the projected colours covering your face like a 1960s LSD trip, and your shadow blocking key components of the slide.

However, this shouldn't be confused with diving into the light of the projector to highlight, purposefully, an element of your slide that should be highlighted. Standing away from your slide and saying, 'As you can see...' without indicating which section of the slide they're talking about can be ineffective and annoying. So, for example, if you have an image of a scattergraph, don't say, 'As you can see, this cluster proves my point', step into the light and use your hands to show the cluster.

(c) Hans Rosling (TED/leslieimage.com)

Don't swim the English Channel in the light of the projector, just hop into the plunge pool when you need to focus on a point.

Principle 4: Build chunk structure into your slides

Just as a screenplay is written before a movie is made, it helps to create a speech outline *before* creating your slides. That way you can embed the chunk structure in the slides to keep both you and your listeners on track. Effortlessly. With the messages and turning points reflected in your slides, you'll have a guiding hand showing you what to emphasise and when.

Below are three different variations showing how you can use different visual expressions within slides and still reflect the chunk structure. Feel free to combine them to suit your preferences.

1. **The Classic Style**: Bullet points, headings, images, etc.

2. **The Zen Style**: No bullet points and a focus on images. This style is outlined beautifully in the book *Presentation Zen*. Each slide has a key point, while you explain the details verbally. In other words, *remove* clutter so that only the point/message remains. Consider enlarging your images to cover the entire slide and add your point/message as text within that image. This style can still be built around your structure.

3. **The Signpost Style**: Use slides for only the key components of your talk. For example, slides only at the start and the end. Or have slides for just 1 or 2 images or charts you want to explain. Or, slides for title, overview, chunk heading and key point. In between, you can have black slides or hit the 'B' key. This style gives you great freedom to tell stories or interact with the audience, but you have a slide ready when you want to make a point or end your talk.

1. The Classic style

The Classic Bullet points	**Overview** • Chunk 1 heading • Chunk 2 heading • Chunk 3 heading
1	2
Chunk 1 heading • Examples… • Stories… • Great explanations… • ** Have as many slides within each chunk as you please.	**Chunk 1 heading** Key Point for Chunk 1
3	4
Chunk 2 heading • Examples… • Stories… • Great explanations… • ** Have as many slides within each chunk as you please.	**Chunk 2 heading** Key Point for Chunk 2
5	6
Chunk 3 heading • Examples… • Stories… • Great explanations… • ** Have as many slides within each chunk as you please.	**Chunk 3 heading** Key Point for Chunk 3
7	8

2. The Zen style

3. The Signpost style

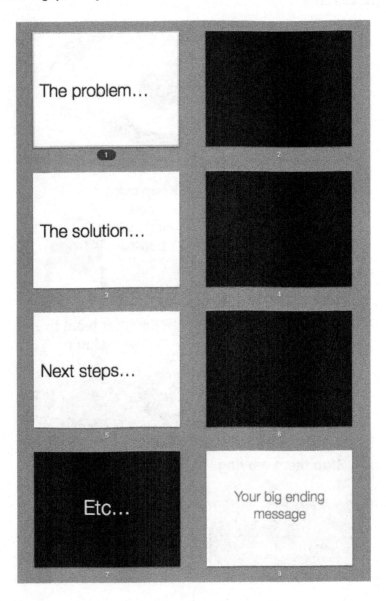

Should you have a final slide with your message?

It's your choice to have a slide at the end for your message. Perhaps you list a few words to help remember it. Or, if it's short enough (like Steve Jobs' 4-word message, 'Stay hungry, stay foolish'), you can have the whole thing on the slide. Or, hit the 'B' key to blank the screen and deliver your message from memory. The choice is yours.

There are many options for the use of slides. These are just a few examples to get you thinking.

No slides - Jim Collins example

I recently saw Jim Collins speak live (author of *Built to Last, Good to Great* and *Great by Choice*). He was terrific. He used no slides at all. During the break, I was chatting with an IT expert about slides versus no slides. He thought it was fantastic to see a speaker who didn't use PowerPoint. He said that, in the IT industry, virtually every presentation is *dominated* by PowerPoint. So he asked whether we should dump slides altogether.

When used without thought, PowerPoint can overpower speakers to the point that, after watching three or four speakers in a row, they all seem similar because their use of presentation software is so similar. So he found it quite refreshing to see a speaker with no slides.

Jim Collins tells fantastic stories, all beautifully held together by his leadership principles. However, if Jim Collins was asking for my feedback (of course, he's not asking for my feedback and seems to be doing fine!), I would recommend some 'Signpost' slides. Perhaps 2 or 3 slides at the *start*, or even just 1 'overview' slide to introduce his topics.

Why? It took the audience a while to understand the scope of his talk, and as a result, it took Jim a while to build momentum and engagement. Slides used solely to create structure at the start can be incredibly effective. They prepare the mind of the listeners in just a few seconds and help them navigate the large amount of content within a long speech. Yet they don't stifle speakers who prefer the freedom to tell stories and connect with their audience without the distraction of a clicker and a screen.

The wrong debate about slides

When I suggest to speakers that they can have just 1 or 2 slides at the start and then none for the rest of their talk, they usually look confused. The whole debate seems to be about ALL ON or ALL OFF -- pick one or the other. The possibilities for visual support are many and varied, yet the common discussion is a narrow black and white debate of should we have slides, yes or no.

The next level of the debate seems to be a choice between the old style PowerPoint template at one end, and the Zen style at the other end, with slides filled with images and very little text. But this is still a narrow, black and white, good/evil discussion.

Bullet points--One word per slide

Text--Images only

The reality is that there is a sliding scale with hundreds of options in between and outside of these 2 perspectives. Don't waste your energy on a debate about slides versus no slides, use your creative awareness to come up with the best combination of visual options to suit your situation. You get to *choose*!

PUBLIC SPEAKING RECAP

So, let's recap the key ideas in this book. There are 3 things that make a great speech.

1. **Message**. *What will they recall that drives your idea into their mind?*

2. **Structure**. *How many sections will you have, what are they called and what's the key point for each?*

3. **Connection**. *Give great explanations in the comfort of your own style.*

By placing your focus on these 3 areas - and away from the *performance rules* - you'll reduce uncertainty and become comfortable in your own skin. And as a result, your anxiety will begin to dissolve. This will effortlessly increase your impact.

SO, TO WRAP UP... BRING YOUR IDEAS TO LIFE!

The word 'vivid' comes from the Latin 'vivere', which means 'alive' or 'to live'. The heart of this book is about *bringing your ideas to life.*

Public speaking was my greatest challenge in the past. I spent years feeling out of control, with thoughts bouncing around like a pinball in an old arcade game. This was true for both *preparation* and *delivery*. It was out of necessity that I developed the Vivid Method. It dissolves obstacles and reveals a simpler path.

Will this method give you the promised **doubling** of impact, while **halving** the effort?

Easily.

In fact, the benefits of pulling away the dark veil from the traditional view of public speaking are much greater. We can now bring our **ideas to life** more easily. There is such a massive difference between *ideas* and the *execution* of ideas. We succeed when we get ideas out of our head and into the minds of others - who can use them and/or share them.

The traditional approach is counterproductive

When presentations are filled with lifeless information, delivered by speakers who are hesitant or full of uncertainty, great ideas are lost as in a fog. The traditional approach feeds this problem by making public speaking seem like a serious, dramatic activity where incomprehensible forces can make you fail or lose control.

But it's not!

- Preparation is not a big, hairy, directionless exploration, it's just a process, guided by your message.

- Anxiety is not a mysterious force that attacks you when you are at your most vulnerable, it's an understandable, observable, natural response to the uncertainty of the spotlight.

- Delivery skills are not a black art that require great acting skills, they are built on breathing comfortably, thinking clearly and being yourself. Recognising this - and having tools to give you clarity and direction - improves your delivery skills effortlessly by opening untapped energy reserves that help bring you to life as you speak.

Ask people: 'What's your message?'

Finally, I encourage you to demand greater clarity from people around you. How? Ask them, *'What's your message?'*

Crisp communication makes a huge difference to the quality of our lives. It helps us manage the growing complexity we must navigate every day. **Vivid messages** and **great explanations** help us sort through the noise, sell ideas and get support for projects. Misunderstandings might be normal, but a lot can be done to win the battle against vague and confusing communication by gently demanding clarity.

Let it be known you expect a concise message. Create a culture in your organisation built on the expectation that each person should be able to answer the question, *'What's your message?'* when proposing an idea or making a presentation.

This can perform communication miracles.

In the meantime, you now have the tools to bring your own ideas to life. The tools are simple, so you can relax and get on with it :)

Bring your idea to life.

Bring your project to life.

Bring your cause to life.

Bring your product to life.

Bring your story to life...

ATTEND THE TRAINING COURSE...

The Vivid Presentation Skills course has been refined and perfected over 10 years. The facilitator creates a fun, stimulating and non-threatening training environment. You'll learn the trusted Vivid Method for public speaking, which demystifies presentation skills and shows you step-by-step how to prepare and deliver compelling presentations.

The course gives you;

1. A simpler way to control nerves.

2. A simpler way to structure your ideas.

3. A simpler way to engage your audience with natural delivery skills.

We can customise this course to focus on your immediate needs. For example, participants have an opportunity to develop a real presentation from start to finish so they are ready to persuade immediately after the course.

Contact Vivid Learning to talk about your needs:
Web: vividmethod.com
Email: events@vividmethod.com
Phone: +61 3 9537 2844

Cam Barber is available for:
- Keynote Speaking
- Conference Sessions
- Messaging Sessions

Index

CPSIA information can be obtained
at www.ICGtesting.com
Printed in the USA
LVOW03s0637101217
559271LV00003B/11/P